AIRMONT SHAKESPEARE CLASSICS SERIES

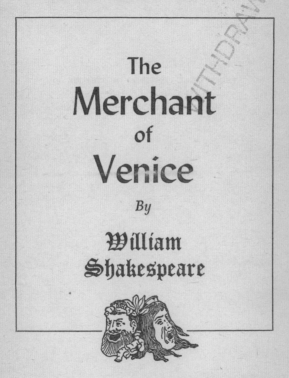

The
Merchant
of
Venice

By

William Shakespeare

AIRMONT PUBLISHING COMPANY, INC.
22 EAST 60TH STREET · NEW YORK 10022

An Airmont Classic
specially selected for the Airmont Library
from the immortal literature of the world

PUBLISHED SIMULTANEOUSLY IN THE DOMINION OF CANADA
BY THE RYERSON PRESS, TORONTO

PRINTED IN THE UNITED STATES OF AMERICA
BY THE COLONIAL PRESS INC., CLINTON, MASSACHUSETTS

PREFACE

For the Airmont series of plays by William Shakespeare, we have chosen a text that we believe more nearly preserves the flavor of the old Shakespearean English than do those of more modernized versions.

In a popular-priced paperback edition, it is almost impossible to include a complete compilation of notes because of the limitations of the format. We suggest that the reader refer to the following excellent textbooks for additional material: *The New Valiorum* (Cambridge and Arden editions); the Oxford edition edited by W. J. Craig (1891); and the editions by G. L. Kittredge (1936). Also, the following books will be helpful to a better understanding of Shakespeare: M. W. McCallum, *Shakespeares' Roman Plays* (1910); Harley Granville-Barker, *Prefaces to Shakespeare, First Series* (London, 1933); John Palmer, *Political Characters of Shakespeare* (London, 1945); Gerald Sanders, *A Shakespeare Primer* (New York and Toronto, 1945); J. Dover Wilson, *The Essential Shakespeare* (London, 1930; New York, 1932).

Dr. David G. Pitt, who wrote the general introduction for each of the plays, received his B.A. degree from Mt. Allison University in New Brunswick, and his M.A. and Ph.D. degrees from the University of Toronto. Since 1949, he has been in the English Department at Memorial University of Newfoundland and Professor of English there since 1962. His publications include articles on literary and educational subjects, and editorial work on Shakespeare.

Ernest Redekop, who wrote the introduction for *The Merchant of Venice*, graduated from the University of Manitoba in 1959 with an Honours Degree in English literature. He studied modern German literature, philosophy and Chaucer at the University of Munich in Germany, and received his Master's degree in 1960 from the University of Toronto. He is presently studying for a doctorate in English at the University of Toronto. He is carrying on research for a Ph.D. thesis on the types of characters in American fiction before the Civil War, pursuing much of this research at Harvard University.

GENERAL INTRODUCTION

William Shakespeare: His Life, Times, and Theatre

HIS LIFE

The world's greatest poet and playwright, often called the greatest Englishman, was born in Stratford-upon-Avon, Warwickshire, in the year 1564. The exact date of his birth is uncertain, but an entry in the *Stratford Parish Register* gives his baptismal date as April 26. Since children were usually baptized two or three days after birth, it is reasonable to assume that he was born on or about April 23—an appropriate day, being the feast of St. George, the patron saint of England.

His father, John Shakespeare, was a glover and dealer in wool and farm products, who had moved to Stratford from Snitterfield, four miles distant, some time before 1552. During his early years in Stratford his business prospered, enabling him to acquire substantial property, including several houses, and to take his place among the more considerable citizens of the town. In 1557 he married Mary, daughter of Robert Arden, a wealthy landowner of Wilmcote, not far from Stratford. Two daughters were born to them before William's birth—Joan, baptized in 1558, and Margaret, baptized in 1562—but both died in infancy. William was thus their third child, though the eldest of those who survived infancy. After him were born Gilbert (1566), another Joan (1569), Anne (1571), Richard (1574), and Edmund (1580).

Very little is positively known (though much is conjectured) about Shakespeare's boyhood and education. We know that for some years after William's birth his father's rise in Stratford society and municipal affairs continued. Many local offices came to him in rapid succession: ale-taster, burgess (a kind of constable), assessor of fines, chamberlain (town treasurer), high bailiff (a kind of magistrate), alderman (town councilor), and chief alderman in 1571. As the son of a man of such eminence in Stratford, Shakespeare undoubtedly attended the local Grammar School. This he was entitled to do free of charge, his father being a town councilor. No records of the school are extant, so that we do not know how good a pupil he was nor what subjects he studied. It is probable that he covered the usual Elizabethan curriculum: an "A B C book," the catechism in Latin and English, Latin grammar, the translation of Latin authors, and perhaps some Greek grammar and translation as well. But family circumstances appear to have curtailed his formal education before it was complete, for shortly before William reached his fourteenth birthday his father's rising fortunes abruptly passed their zenith.

Although we do not know all the facts, it is apparent that about the year 1578, having gone heavily into debt, John Shakespeare lost two large farms inherited by his wife from her father. Thereafter, he was involved in a series of lawsuits, and lost his post on the Stratford town council. Matters got steadily worse for him, until finally in 1586 he was declared a bankrupt. But by this time the future poet-dramatist was already a family man himself.

In 1582, in the midst of his father's legal and financial crises—and perhaps because of them—Shakespeare married Anne, daughter of Richard Hathaway (recently deceased) of the village of Shottery near Stratford. The *Episcopal Register* for the Diocese of Worcester contains their marriage record, dated November 28, 1582; he was then in his eighteenth year and his wife in her twenty-sixth. On May 26 of the following year the *Stratford Parish Register* recorded the baptism of their first child, Susanna; and on February 2, 1585, the baptism of a twin son and daughter named Hammet and Judith.

These facts are all that are known of Shakespeare's early life. How he supported his family, whether he took up some trade or profession, how long he continued to live in Stratford, we do not know for certain. Tradition and conjecture have bestowed on him many interim occupations between his marriage and his appearance in London in the early fifteen-nineties: printer, dyer, traveling-player, butcher, soldier, apothecary, thief—it reads like a children's augury-rhyme (when buttons or cherry-stones are read to learn one's fate). Perhaps only the last-named "pursuit" requires some explanation. According to several accounts, one of them appearing in the first *Life* of Shakespeare by Nicholas Rowe (1709), Shakespeare fell into bad company sometime after his marriage, and on several occasions stole deer from the park of Sir Thomas Lucy, a substantial gentleman of Charlecote, near Stratford. According to Rowe:

> For this he was prosecuted by that gentleman, as he thought somewhat too severely; and in order to revenge that ill-usage, he made a ballad upon him . . . and was obliged to leave his business and family in Warwickshire, for some time, and shelter himself in London.

The story has been repeated in varying forms by most subsequent biographers, but its authenticity is doubted by many who repeat it.

Another much more attractive story, which, however, if true, does not necessarily deny the authenticity of Rowe's, is that Shakespeare during the so-called "lost years" was a schoolmaster. This, indeed, appears to be somewhat better substantiated. John Aubrey, seventeenth-century biographer and antiquary, in his *Brief Lives* (1681) declares that he had learned from a theatrical manager, whose father had known Shakespeare, that the dramatist "had been in his younger years a schoolmaster in the country." This may, then, account, in part at least, for the years between his marriage and his arrival in London about the year 1591. It is interesting to note that in two of his early plays Shakespeare includes a schoolmaster among his characters: Holofernes of *Love's Labour's Lost* and Pinch of *The Comedy of Errors*. But let us hope that neither is intended to be Shakespeare's portrait of himself!

However he may have occupied himself in the interim, we know that by 1592 he was already a budding actor and play-

wright in London. In that year Robert Greene in his auto-
biographical pamphlet *A Groatsworth of Wit*, referring to the
young actors and menders of old plays who were, it seemed
to him, gaining undeserved glory from the labours of their
betters (both by acting their plays and by rewriting them),
wrote as follows:

> Yes trust them not: for there is an upstart Crow, beautified
> with our feathers, that with his Tygers heart wrapt in a
> Players hyde, supposes he is as well able to bombast out
> blanke verse as the best of you: and being an absolute
> *Johannes factotum*, is in his owne conceit the onely Shake-
> scene in a countrey.

"Shakescene" is clearly Shakespeare. The phrase "upstart
Crow" probably refers to his country origins and his lack
of university education. "Beautified with our feathers" probably means that he uses the other playwrights' words for his
own aggrandisement either in plays in which he acts or in
those he writes himself. "Tygers heart wrapt in a Players
hyde" is a parody of a line in III *Henry VI*, one of the
earliest plays ascribed to Shakespeare. And the Latin phrase
Johannes factotum, meaning Jack-of-all-trades, suggests that
he was at this time engaged in all sorts of theatrical jobs:
actor, poet, playwright, and perhaps manager as well.

Greene died shortly after making this scurrilous attack on
the young upstart from Stratford, and so escaped the resent-
ment of those he had insulted. But Henry Chettle, himself
a minor dramatist, who had prepared Greene's manuscript
for the printer, in his *Kind-Harts Dreame* (1592), apologized
to Shakespeare for his share in the offence:

> I am as sory as if the original fault had beene my fault, be-
> cause my selfe have seene his demeanor no lesse civill, than
> he excelent in the qualitie he professes: Besides, divers
> of worship have reported his uprightness of dealing, which
> argues honesty, and his facetious grace in writing, that
> approoves his Art.

Thus, in very indirect manner and because of an attack upon
him by an irascible dying man, we learn that Shakespeare

at this time was in fact held in high regard by "divers of worship," that is, by many of high birth, as an upright, honest young man of pleasant manners and manifest skill as actor, poet, and playwright.

Although Shakespeare by 1593 had written, or written parts of, some five or six plays (I, II, and III *Henry VI*, *Richard III*, *The Comedy of Errors*, and perhaps *Titus Andronicus*), it was as a non-dramatic poet that he first appeared in print. *Venus and Adonis* and *The Rape of Lucrece*, long narrative poems, both bearing Shakespeare's name, were published in 1593 and 1594 respectively. But thereafter for the next twenty years he wrote almost nothing but drama. In his early period, 1591 to 1596, in addition to the plays named above he wrote *Love's Labour's Lost*, *The Taming of the Shrew*, *Two Gentlemen of Verona*, *Romeo and Juliet*, *A Midsummer Night's Dream*, *Richard II*, and *King John*. Then followed his great middle period, 1596 to 1600, during which he wrote both comedies and history-plays: *The Merchant of Venice*, I and II *Henry IV*, *The Merry Wives of Windsor*, *Much Ado about Nothing*, *Henry V*, *Julius Caesar*, *As You Like It*, and *Twelfth Night*. The period of his great tragedies and the so-called "dark comedies" followed (1600-1608): *Hamlet*, *Troilus and Cressida*, *All's Well that Ends Well*, *Measure for Measure*, *Othello*, *King Lear*, *Macbeth*, *Antony and Cleopatra*, *Timon of Athens*, and *Coriolanus*. The last phase of his career as dramatist, 1608 to 1613, sometimes called "the period of the romances," produced *Pericles, Prince of Tyre*, *Cymbeline*, *The Winter's Tale*, *The Tempest*, parts of *Henry VIII*, and perhaps parts of *The Two Noble Kinsmen*. Many other plays were ascribed to him, but it is doubtful that he had a hand in any but those we have named. Long before his death in 1616 his name held such magic for the public that merely to print it on the title page of any play assured its popular acclaim. The "upstart Crow" had come a long way since 1592.

He had come a long way too from the economic straits that may well have driven him to London many years before. We know, for example, from the records of tax assessments that by 1596 Shakespeare was already fairly well-to-do. This is further borne out by his purchasing in the following year a substantial house known as New Place and an acre of land in Stratford for £60, a sizable sum in those days. In 1602 he made a further purchase of 107 acres at Stratford for £320, and a cottage and more land behind his estate at New Place. But his life during this time was not quite unclouded. His only son, Hamnet, died in 1596 at the age of eleven years, his father in 1601, and his mother in 1608. All three were buried in Stratford. More happily he saw, in 1607, the marriage of his daughter Susanna to Dr. John Hall, an eminent physician of Stratford, and, in the following year, the baptism of his granddaughter, Elizabeth Hall.

Shakespeare's retirement to Stratford appears to have been gradual, but by 1613, if not earlier, he seems to have settled there, though he still went up to London occasionally. Of the last months of his life we know little. We do know that in February, 1616, his second daughter, Judith, married Thomas Quiney. We know that on March 25, apparently already ill, Shakespeare revised and signed his will, among other bequests leaving to his wife his "second best bed with the furniture." A month later he was dead, dying on his fifty-second birthday, April 23, 1616. He was buried in the chancel of Holy Trinity Church, Stratford, on April 26.

HIS TIMES

Shakespeare lived during the English Renaissance, that age of transition that links the Mediaeval and the Modern world. Inheriting the rich traditions of the Middle Ages in art, learning, religion, and politics, rediscovering the great legacies of classical culture, the men of the Renaissance went on to new and magnificent achievements in every phase of human endeavour. No other period in history saw such varied and prolific development and expansion. And the reign of Elizabeth I (1558-1603), Shakespeare's age, was the High Renaissance in England.

Development and expansion—these are the watchwords of

the age, and they apply to every aspect of life, thought, and activity. The universe grew in immensity as men gradually abandoned the old Ptolemaic view of a finite, earth-centered universe, accepting the enormous intellectual challenge of the illimitable cosmos of Copernicus's theory and Galileo's telescope. The earth enlarged, too, as more of its surface was discovered and charted by explorers following the lead of Columbus, Cabot, Magellan, and Vespucci. England itself expanded as explorers and colonizers, such as Frobisher, Davis, Gilbert, Raleigh, Grenville, Drake, and others, carried the English flag into many distant lands and seas; as English trade and commerce expanded with the opening of new markets and new sources of supply; as English sea power grew to protect the trading routes and fend off rivals, particularly Spain, the defeat of whose Invincible Armada in 1588 greatly advanced English national pride at home, and power and prestige abroad.

The world of ideas changed and expanded, too. The rediscovery and reinterpretation of the classics, with their broad and humane view of life, gave a new direction and impetus to secular education. During the Middle Ages theology had dominated education, but now the language, literature, and philosophy of the ancient world, the practical arts of grammar, logic, and rhetoric, and training in morals, manners, and gymnastics assumed the major roles in both school and university—in other words, an education that fitted one for life in the world here and now replaced one that looked rather to the life hereafter. Not that the spiritual culture of man was neglected. Indeed, it took on a new significance, for as life in this world acquired new meaning and value, religion assumed new functions, and new vitality to perform them, as the bond between the Creator and a new kind of creation.

It was, of course, the old creation—man and nature—but it was undergoing great changes. Some of these we have already seen, but the greatest was in man's conception of himself and his place in nature. The Mediaeval view of man was generally not an exalted one. It saw him as more or

less depraved, fallen from Grace as a result of Adam's sin;
and the things of this world, which was also "fallen," as of
little value in terms of his salvation. Natural life was thought
of mainly as a preparation for man's entry into Eternity. But
Renaissance thought soon began to rehabilitate man, nature,
and the things of this life. Without denying man's need for
Grace and the value of the means of salvation provided by
the Church, men came gradually to accept the idea that
there were "goods", values, "innocent delights" to be had in
the world here and now, and that God had given them for
man to enjoy. Man himself was seen no longer as wholly
vile and depraved, incapable even of desiring goodness, but
rather as Shakespeare saw him in *Hamlet*:

> What a piece of work is man! how noble in reason! how
> infinite in faculty! in form and moving how express and ad-
> mirable! in action how like an angel! in apprehension how
> like a god! the beauty of the world! the paragon of animals!

And this is the conception of man that permeates Elizabethan thought and literature. It does not mean that man
is incorruptible, immune to moral weakness and folly. Shakespeare has his villains, cowards, and fools. But man is none
of these by nature; they are distortions of the true form of
man. Nature framed him for greatness, endowed him with
vast capacities for knowledge, achievement, and delight, and
with aspirations that may take him to the stars. "O brave
new world, That has such people in 't!"

The chief object of man's aspiring mind is now the natural
world, whose "wondrous architecture," says Marlowe's Tam-
burlaine, our souls strive ceaselessly to comprehend, "Still
climbing after knowledge infinite." Hamlet, too, speaks of "this
goodly frame, the earth . . . this brave o'erhanging firmament,
this majestical roof fretted with golden fire." No longer the
ruins of a fallen paradise and the devil's, nature is seen as
man's to possess, her beauty and wonder to be sought after
and enjoyed, her energies to be controlled and used—as
Bacon expressed it, "for the glory of the Creator and the relief
of man's estate."

It was, indeed, a very stirring time to be alive in. New vistas were breaking upon the human mind and imagination everywhere. It was a time like spring, when promise, opportunity, challenge and growth appeared where none had been dreamed of before. Perhaps this is why there is so much poetry of springtime in the age of Shakespeare.

HIS THEATRE

There were many theatres, or playhouses, in Shakespeare's London. The first was built in 1576 by James Burbage and was called the *Theatre*. It was built like an arena, with a movable platform at one end, and had no seats in the pit, but had benches in the galleries that surrounded it. It was built of wood, and cost about £200. Other famous playhouses of Shakespeare's time, for the most part similarly constructed, included the Curtain, the Bull, the Rose, the Swan, the Fortune, and, most famous of them all, the Globe. It was built in 1599 by the sons of James Burbage, and it was here that most of Shakespeare's plays were performed. Since more is known about the Globe than most of the others, I shall use it as the basis of the brief account that follows of the Elizabethan playhouse.

As its name suggests the Globe was a circular structure (the second Globe, built in 1614 after the first burned down, was octagonal), and was open to the sky, somewhat like a modern football or baseball stadium, though much smaller. It had three tiers of galleries surrounding the central "yard" or pit, and a narrow roof over the top gallery. But most interesting from our viewpoint was the stage—or rather *stages*—which was very different from that of most modern theatres. These have the familiar "picture-frame" stage: a raised platform at one end of the auditorium, framed by curtains and footlights, and viewed only from the front like a picture. Shakespeare's stage was very different.

The main stage, or *apron* as it was called, jutted well out into the pit, and did not extend all the way across from side to side. There was an area on either side for patrons to sit or stand in, so that actors performing on the apron could be viewed from three sides instead of one. In addition there was an inner stage, a narrow rectangular recess let into the wall behind the main stage. When not in use it could be closed by a curtain drawn across in front; when open it could be used for interior scenes, arbor scenes, tomb and anteroom scenes and the like. On either side of this inner stage were doors through which the main stage was entered. Besides the inner and outer stages there were no fewer than four other areas where the action of the play, or parts of it, might be performed. Immediately above the inner stage, and corresponding to it in size and shape, was another room with its front exposed. This was the upper stage, and was used for upstairs scenes, or for storage when not otherwise in use. In front of this was a narrow railed gallery, which could be used for balcony scenes, or ones requiring the walls of a castle or the ramparts of a fortress. On either side of it and on the same level was a window-stage, so-called because it consisted of a small balcony enclosed by windows that opened on hinges. This permitted actors to stand inside and speak from the open windows to others on the main stage below. In all it was a very versatile multiple stage and gave the dramatist and producer much more freedom in staging than most modern theatres afford. It is interesting to note that some of the new theatres today have revived certain of the features of the Elizabethan stage.

Very little in the way of scenery and backdrops was used. The dramatist's words and the imagination of the audience supplied the lack of scenery. No special lighting effects were possible since plays were performed in the daylight that streamed in through the unroofed top of the three-tiered enclosure that was the playhouse. Usually a few standard stage-props were on hand: trestles and boards to form a table, benches and chairs, flagons, an altar, artificial trees, weapons, a man's severed head, and a few other items. Costumes were usually elaborate and gorgeous, though no attempt was made to reproduce the dress of the time and place portrayed in the play.

Play production in Shakespeare's time was clearly very different from that of ours, but we need have no doubts about the audience's response to what they saw and heard on stage. They came, they saw, and the dramatist conquered, for they kept coming back for more and more. And despite the opposition that the theatre encountered from Puritans and others, who thought it the instrument of Satan, the theatre in Shakespeare's time flourished as one of the supreme glories of a glorious age.

–DAVID G. PITT
*Memorial University of
Newfoundland.*

INTRODUCTION TO
The Merchant of Venice

The Merchant of Venice is a gambler. He bets a pound of his flesh that a half-dozen ships of his will return in time to pay a debt to a moneylender. It is a dangerous gamble; but he does this out of pure friendship for Bassanio, who is also a gambler: Bassanio bets the small fortune he has borrowed from Antonio that he will win a beautiful lady and her large fortune. Bassanio wins; Antonio almost loses—but not quite. At the crucial moment, when justice appears most relentless and fortune most indifferent, tragedy is averted. "The most excellent Historie of the *Merchant of Venice,*" as the play is called on the title page of the text of 1600, turns out to be a comedy. The fortunes of Antonio descend to a threatening nadir, then rise again. The villain, who seems to be triumphing, is caught in the tangles of his own trap. *The Merchant of Venice*, however, is much more complicated than this. Antonio does not dominate the stage like the heroes of Shakespeare's tragedies, and Shylock, thorough villain that he is, can still arouse some sympathy.

OPPOSING CONCEPTS OF WEALTH

Onstage the role of Shylock tends to overshadow the others, and a balance must be kept between the hatred of Shylock for Antonio on the one hand and the friendship between Antonio and Bassanio on the other. The difference between these two kinds of relationship derives largely from a difference in ideas about the nature of wealth. To Shylock, wealth means money—money for its own sake. He loves money passionately. When he has to make a choice between his daughter and his ducats, we have no doubt about his first love: "Would she were dead at my foot, and the ducats in her coffin," he says of Jessica after her elopement.

All the major characters in this play have made a choice, at one point or another, between human love and friendship and dehumanizing love of riches. It is not surprising that in a play about a merchant the language and action are often mercantile, that the exchange of money is an important symbol. Even love is sometimes expressed in commercial imagery: "Since you are dear bought," says Portia to Bassanio, "I will love you dear." For Portia, however, money is only a means, an instrument; for Shylock it is the object of a passion that can only be displaced temporarily by the stronger passions of hatred and desire for revenge. Even these passions are based ultimately on his avarice. Shylock hates Antonio, he says, because the merchant is a Christian;

> But more, for that, in low simplicity,
> He lends out money gratis, and brings down
> The rate of usance here with us in Venice. (I, iii, p. 18)

Not only does Antonio harm Shylock's business; he also insults him by railing on him, on his bargains, and on his "well-won thrift." Shylock's hero is Jacob who, exercising hard-headed enterprise and helped by an accommodating God, managed to breed only spotted lambs and build up his own flocks by tricking his master, Laban. Contrasted with Shylock's cupidity is Antonio's generosity:

> . . . be assured
> My purse, my person, my extremest means,
> Lie all unlockt to your occasions, (I, i, p. 8)

he tells Bassanio. For Antonio, friendship is more significant than cash; he lends and gives freely to Bassanio without security or interest. From Shylock he cannot expect the same:

> If thou wilt lend this money, lend it not
> As to thy friends—for when did friendship take
> A breed for barren metal of his friend?—
> But lend it rather to thine enemy;
> Who if he break, thou mayst with better face
> Exact the penalty. (I, iii, p. 21)

For a moment, Shylock seems to accept Antonio's idea of money:

I would be friends with you . . .

. . . .

                            . . . and take no doit
Of usance for my moneys,
     And you'll not hear me: this is kind I offer.
                              (I, iii, p. 21)

That Shylock is quite hypocritical in pretending friendship,
however, is clear from his aside earlier in this scene, as
well as from Bassanio's distrust here. "This were kindness,"
answers Bassanio; indeed it would be kindness if Shylock were
to be trusted—but trust him Bassanio cannot:

     You shall not seal to such a bond for me:
     I'll rather dwell in my necessity, (I, iii, p. 22)

he says to Antonio, warning him that he does not "like . . .
fair terms, and a villain's mind."

REVENGE AND THE BOND

That Shylock is a villain cannot really be doubted, if the
play is acted or read with care. Actors like Edmund Kean and
Henry Irving raised Shylock above the level of a grasping
ogre, but excited perhaps too much sympathy for an antag-
onist "no less sinned against than sinning," as William Hazlitt
said in recalling Kean's Shylock of 1817. Is Shylock indeed
justified in his revenge? The answer is, I think, no. His hatred
of Antonio is rooted partly in religious distrust, partly in
Antonio's scorn for usurers and Jews, and it is increased by
the elopement of his daughter. It is rooted most deeply, however, as I have tried to show, in the difference beween Shylock's and Antonio's concepts of money and in Shylock's
bitter envy of Antonio's financial power. Antonio's ill-usage
of Shylock (notorious to modern audiences) arises from
disgust at Shylock's avaricious lending of money at high rates
of interest. Shylock hates Antonio for this scorn; he hates
him more because this scorn is not only verbal, like Gratiano's.
The bond is not "a merry sport," nor does Shylock only determine to exact the pound of flesh after his daughter's elopement. When he parts with Launcelot—before Jessica leaves
—he says to her:

> . . . drones hive not with me;
> Therefore I part with him; and part with him
> To one that I would have him help to waste
> His borrow'd purse. (II, v, p. 43)

These are not the words of a man anxious for the safe return of his three thousand ducats. Behind this sentence of Shylock's is faith in a long gamble—that all of Antonio's six ships will, for some reason or other (because of "land-rats, and water-rats, water-thieves, and land-thieves," or "the peril of waters, winds and rocks," as Shylock says), fail to make port before the bond expires, and that he will get his dearly bought pound of flesh. His hatred of Antonio and his determination to have revenge are evident from the beginning and are only increased when he discovers that his daughter is missing—more significantly, that his gold and his jewels are gone. These are uppermost in his mind, and the same love of money underlies his exclamations when Salarino asks him "whether Antonio have had any loss at sea or no?"

> There I have another bad match, a bankrout, a prodigal, who dare scarce show his head on the Rialto;—a beggar, that was used to come so smug upon the mart;—let him look to his bond; he was wont to call me usurer;—let him look to his bond: he was wont to lend money for a Christian courtesy:—let him look to his bond. (III, i, pp. 60-61)

Shylock's reiteration of "let him look to his bond" anticipates his fourfold repetition of "I'll have my bond" when he meets Antonio in the street before the trial. Antonio very simply expresses the reason for this implacable hatred:

> I oft deliver'd from his forfeitures
> Many that have at times made moan to me;
> Therefore he hates me. (III, iii, p. 78)

Earlier in the same act, in his conversation with Salarino and Solanio, Shylock explains his motives for revenge in his most sophistical speech, a speech often misinterpreted as Shakespeare's plea for a humanitarian attitude toward Jews. It is nothing of the sort. Note Salarino's question: "Why I am sure, if he forfeit, thou wilt not take his flesh; what's that good for?", which recalls Shylock's hypocritical reasoning in Act I:

> If he should break his day, what should I gain
> By the exaction of the forfeiture?
> A pound of man's flesh taken from a man
> Is not so estimable, profitable neither,
> As flesh of muttons, beefs, or goats . . . (I, iii, p. 22)

In Act III, Shylock drops all pretense; a man's flesh is now indeed "estimable" to him—it is good "To bait fish withal; if it will feed nothing else, it will feed my revenge." Antonio, he says, "hath disgraced me, and hinder'd me half a million; laught at my losses, mockt at my gains, scorn'd my nation, thwarted my bargains, cooled my friends, heated mine enemies . . ." (III, i, p. 61). And he has done this, says Shylock, because "I am a Jew." The following lines are indeed an indictment of Christians in their attitude toward the Jews; but they are not the outcry of a noble member of a downtrodden race. Shylock's speech is not a touching plea for sympathy. It is a malicious argument for revenge:

> If a Jew wrong a Christian, what is his humility? revenge:
> if a Christian wrong a Jew, what should his sufferance be
> by Christian example? why, revenge. The villainy you
> teach me, I will execute; and it shall go hard but I will
> better the instruction. (III, i, p. 61)

Shylock is the last person to need such instruction. Secure in the overriding power of Venetian law, he even refuses to give the Duke any good reason for his "strange apparent cruelty," comparing his hatred of Antonio to the loathing of one man for a rat, of another for a pig, of others for a cat or a bagpipe. And unfeeling as the attitude of the Christians to the Jews may have been, the "instruction" in the trial scene is directed toward the exercise of mercy rather than toward insistence on the letter of the law. Portia gives Shylock three chances to retract and eloquently pleads with him to show mercy. The Duke, despite the open rapacity of Shylock, is generous:

That thou shalt see the difference of our spirits,
I pardon thee thy life before thou ask it . . . (IV, i, p. 104)

Antonio, too, in spite of our abhorrence of the demand that
Shylock turn Christian, would have been considered both
merciful and generous by an Elizabethan audience whose
immediate contact with Jews was probably limited to the sen-
sational hanging, drawing, and quartering of a Portuguese Jew,
Roderigo Lopez, some two years before the first performance
of *The Merchant of Venice*. Many Elizabethan playgoers
would have considered the forcible conversion of a Jew an
act of mercy, and certainly they would have been much less
impressed than Shylock with the harshness of a fine imposed
on a usurer.

WEALTH AND THE VENETIANS

Contrasted with Shylock, usury and the love of money for
its own sake, are the Venetians and Portia. For Shylock, wealth
means getting and keeping. His house is the center and substance of his life; after the sentence has been passed, he says
despairingly to the Duke:

Nay, take my life and all; pardon not that:
You take my house, when you do take the prop
That doth sustain my house; you take my life,
When you do take the means whereby I live. (IV, i, p. 105)

For Antonio and Bassanio, wealth means getting and giving.
Bassanio, in choosing the lead casket, gives and hazards all
he has. So does Antonio in giving Bassanio money he has
borrowed on the security of his own body. Salarino thinks
Antonio is melancholy because his mind "is tossing on the
ocean," and Solanio imagines his own apprehension if he had
ships like Antonio's. But material investments are not uppermost in Antonio's mind, and the concern of his friends for
the safe return of his ships, intensified by recurring references
to their possible loss, is not commercial, but personal. Antonio
places his friendship to Bassanio before all else, generously
forgiving him all his debts when it begins to appear that
Shylock will have the forfeit, and quite as generously placing

Bassanio's present happiness with Portia before his own desire to see him once more before his death.

Both Antonio and Bassanio are what Shylock calls "prodigal," the merchant for spending money freely for his friend, Bassanio for being a spendthrift with another's money. This Venetian society does not live by the wisdom of Midas or the logic of Shylock. Bassanio's argument about shooting a second arrow may be illogical, but in this story his atempt to regain Antonio's money does succeed. Not entirely because of his own good sense and fortune, however. Portia, too, has the noble attitude toward wealth:

> You see me, Lord Bassanio, where I stand,
> Such as I am: though for myself alone
> I would not be ambitious in my wish,
> To wish myself much better; yet for you
> I would be trebled twenty times myself;
> A thousand times more fair, ten thousand times more rich;
> That, only to stand high in your account,
> I might in virtues, beauties, livings, friends,
> Exceed account . . . (III, ii, pp. 69-70)

There is no hesitation in her magnificent offer to Bassanio "to pay the petty debt twenty times over."

WISDOM AND THE CASKETS

Such an attitude toward riches in one who has much is no isolated expression of character. The whole point of the casket story is the success of the suitor who despises material riches for their own sake and accordingly sees past appearances to truth, who is as willing to "give and hazard" all he has as to get. Morocco fails because he considers gold the only adequate setting for such a gem as the Lady of Belmont. Like Shylock, he thinks of gold as precious in itself; he judges its worth by its appearance. This is folly; it is toying with death, and Morocco's reward is a skull with appropriate verses. Arragon, too, judges by appearances, although he thinks he is prying "to th' interior." His reasoning is perhaps a bit more subtle, but the images he uses show that the honor he admires is still externally marked: honor should have "the stamp of merit"; it should be able to "stand bare"; if it "were purchased by the merit of the wearer," much honor would be "pickt from the chaff and ruin of the times, / To be new-varnisht!"—that is, to regain a new *appearance* of nobility. Arragon does not go beyond an appreciation of own apparent merit: "I will assume desert," he says. This, as he discovers to his chagrin, is the assumption of "a blinking idiot." Only Bassanio chooses rightly. He reflects wisely:

> So may the outward shows be least themselves:
> The world is still deceived with ornament . . .
>> (III, ii, p. 67)

Corruptions and errors in law and religion may be hidden by a "gracious voice" or a "sober brow"; virtues may be "assumed" (as the Prince of Arragon assumed merit); beauty may be an illusion. Bassanio sees *into* things, as he has seen into Shylock and his hypocritical generosity. In doing so, he gains his "fortune," as he reads in the scroll. Again the metaphor is commercial: Bassanio has "come by note, to give and to receive." He is "doubtful whether what I see be true, / Until confirm'd, sign'd, ratified by you," he says to Portia. Bassanio both gives and receives, and so this I. O. U. is related to the motto on the lead casket. He imagines a financial transaction that is the diametric opposite of Shylock's bond; he has found his "thrift" (I, i, p. 10) not only in Portia's beauty and wealth but also in her virtues.

THE CACOPHONY OF GREED AND THE HARMONY OF LOVE

Shylock's "thrift," on the other hand, is the monetary gain of a sober and acquisitive Puritan, of a calculating man utterly devoid of poetry. Hearing from Launcelot that a masque will take place on the night of Bassanio's feast, he tells Jessica to

> Lock up my doors; and when you hear the drum,
> And the vile squealing of the wry-neckt fife,
> Clamber not you up to the casements then,
> Nor thrust your head into the public street,
> To gaze on Christian fools with varnisht faces;
> But stop my house's ears, I mean my casements:

Let not the sound of shallow foppery enter
My sober house. (II, v, p. 42)

For Bassanio, however, Portia commands music and he makes his choice of caskets to the accompaniment of a song. At Belmont, Lorenzo and Jessica (who loves her husband with an "unthrift love") are sensitive to "the touches of sweet harmony" and can imagine the music of the spheres. Music, says Lorenzo, can turn the "savage eyes" of wild colts chased by mad hounds to a "modest gaze":

> . . . therefore the poet
> Did feign that Orpheus drew trees, stones, and floods;
> Since naught so stockish, hard, and full of rage,
> But music for the time doth change his nature . . .
> (V, i, p. 116)

Over Shylock, however, Orpheus can have no power. He is indeed the cur he is called. In the trial scene Antonio compares him in his stubbornness to the "main flood" at its height, to a wolf, to mountain pines caught in the wind. Nothing can be harder than Shylock's heart. He is all the hard and raging things of nature that Orpheus could tame— but he is quite deaf to Orpheus' lute:

> The man that hath no music in himself,
> Nor is not moved with concord of sweet sounds,
> Is fit for treasons, stratagems, and spoils;
> The motions of his spirit are dull as night,
> And his affections dark as Erebus:
> Let no such man be trusted.—(V, i, pp. 116-117)

says Lorenzo to Jessica. He could have been thinking of Shylock, whose incessant cries for justice and his bond have sounded a cacophony of greed through Venice. Here at Belmont, in the quiet of night, order is finally restored and the play ends in a harmony of love.

ERNEST REDEKOP, M.A.
Trinity College, Toronto

STUDY QUESTIONS

ACT I

1. In the first act of this play two stories are introduced, the bond story and the casket story. How does Shakespeare relate them to each other in this act?

2. How is the audience prepared for the seriousness of Antonio's gamble?

3. Compare Shylock's use of language with that of the Venetians, noting especially the use of images, metaphors, repetition and so on. What can you tell about Shylock, Bassanio, Gratiano and the other Venetians from their language?

4. What was the Elizabethan attitude toward usury? Trace the official and unofficial Christian attitudes, up to Shakespeare's time, toward lending money for interest.

5. Write preliminary character sketches of Antonio, Bassanio, Shylock and Portia.

6. Read the story of Jacob and Laban in the Book of Genesis and say whether or not Shylock is justified in arguing for usury as he does.

ACT II

1. How does Shakespeare use comedy in this act? Compare Launcelot to one other clown or fool in Shakespeare's plays. Is his role necessary?

2. Note all the references to external appearance and internal reality. Keeping these in mind, how are the Prince of Morocco, the Prince of Arragon,

the three caskets, the half-blind father of Launcelot, Jessica and Shylock related?

3. Discuss the relationship of friendship to money.

4. Are the arguments of Morocco and Arragon reasonable? Do they deserve their fates?

5. Why does Shylock not appear onstage in scene
viii of this act? Why are his actions and words
reported and not acted?

6. What relevance does Lorenzo's abduction of
Nerissa have to the main plot?

ACT III

1. Is Shylock's long speech to Salarino in Scene i a
plea for tolerance or a sophistical argument for
revenge? Give reasons for your answer, relating
the speech to the character of Shylock as a whole.

2. Relating your answer to Question 2 of Act II, discuss the significance of Bassanio's choice.

3. Note the language of Antonio's letter to Bassanio
and compare it to Shylock's rhetoric in talking to
Antonio in scene iii.

4. Characterize Portia from the descriptions of her
by other characters.

5. How does Shakespeare continue to relate the bond
and casket stories?

6. According to Antonio's letter, at least three months
must have passed since Bassanio left him. Yet
Belmont is at no great distance from Venice and
Bassanio has wasted no time in making his choice
of caskets. How do you account for this dis-
crepancy in time? Is it important onstage? Can
you make a distinction between simple chrono-
logical time and dramatic time, and if so, what
is it?

ACT IV

1. Show in what way Act IV may be considered the climax of the play. At what point in Act IV is the high point reached?

2. Can you reconcile Portia's speech on "the quality of mercy" with her later statement to Shylock: "Thou shalt have justice, more than thou desirest"? Is Portia being hypocritical? Give reasons for your answer.

3. Show how Shylock, step by step, cuts himself off from any hope of mercy. Trace, similarly, his fall from the highest moment of his triumph.

4. Describe the role of Gratiano in this act.

5. Imagining yourself as an Elizabethan seeing the first performance of this play around 1596, discuss the justice of the Duke's treatment of Shylock and the fairness of Antonio's demands.

6. During Shakespeare's time, the roles of women were played by boys. What would the reaction of an Elizabethan audience have been to Portia disguised as a boy in the court scene? Compare Portia's disguise to similar disguises in two other Shakespearean plays.

7. How does Shakespeare use dramatic irony in both scenes of this act?

ACT V

1. Lorenzo says Jessica stole "from the wealthy Jew,/And with an unthrift love did run from Venice. . . ." Why is "unthrift" a good adjective to use for Jessica's love?

2. Contrast Lorenzo's praise of music with Shylock's attitude toward "the vile squealing of the wry-

neck'd fife" in II, v. What is the significance of this contrast?

3. Discuss the imagery of light in this act.

4. When Bassanio chooses the lead casket, the dialogue between him and Portia is elevated and stylized. In Act V, however, the conversation between men and women is quite different, vigorous and at times bawdy. Discuss the differences in tone between III, ii and V, and explain how these differences are achieved.

5. In some stage versions of the play the court scene has been the last. Is this a good or a poor interpretation of the play? What is the dramatic purpose of the last act? How does Shakespeare, after the climax of the court scene, stimulate the attention and interest of an audience right to the very end?

GENERAL QUESTIONS

1. If you can find a translation, read Ser Giovanni's *Il Pecorone*, and compare this possible source with Shakespeare's play. How, in particular, does Shakespeare's Portia differ from the Lady of Belmonte?

2. Trace the development of five of the following themes, motifs and images through the play: appearances vs. truth, Jason and the Golden Fleece, wealth, money, gold, jewels, debt, wagers and music.

3. When does Shakespeare use prose and when verse in this play? Can you discover a pattern? If so, say why he uses these forms as he does.

4. What is the effect of the constant shifting of scene from Venice to Belmont and back again? Are Venice and Belmont, in your opinion, sufficiently

distinct from each other? If so, how are they distinguished from each other and what meaning do they add as contrasted settings to the play?

5. If you were directing a production of this play, how would you want Shylock characterized?

6. Discuss the roles of Solanio and Salarino.

7. Shylock is a comic figure who arouses some sympathy in the onlooker; he remains, however, essentially the butt of our laughter. Write an essay defending or attacking this statement.

8. Could the title "Merchant of Venice" be used to describe Bassanio or Shylock as well as Antonio? Defend your answer.

9. Write brief paragraphs on each of the following passages. Identify the passage within the text, say who is speaking and to whom, and discuss its significance to the play as a whole and for our understanding of the character of the speaker:

   a) Repent but you that you shall lose your friend,
      And he repents not that he pays your debt;
      For, if the Jew do cut but deep enough,
      I'll pay it instantly with all my heart.

   b) Thus ornament is but the guiled shore
      To a most dangerous sea: the beauteous scarf
      Veiling an Indian beauty; in a word,
      The seeming truth which cunning times put on
      To entrap the wisest.

   c) Go with me to a notary, seal me there
      Your single bond; and, in a merry sport,
      If you repay me not on such a day,
      In such a place, such sum or sums as are
      Expresst in the condition, let the forfeit
      Be nominated for an equal pound
      Of your fair flesh. . . .

   d)   . . . thy currish spirit

   Govern'd a wolf, who, hang'd for human
       slaughter—
   Even from the gallows did his fell soul fleet,
   And, whilst thou lay'st in thy unhallow'd
       dam,
   Infused itself in thee; for thy desires
   Are wolvish, bloody, starved, and ravenous.

e) Why, if two gods should play some heavenly
       match,
   And on the wager lay two earthly women,
   And Portia one, there must be something else
   Pawn'd with the other, for the poor rude
       world
   Hath not her fellow.

f) Truly, the more to blame he; we were Christians enow before, e'en as many as could
   well live, one by another. This making of
   Christians will raise the price of hogs: if we
   grow all to be pork-eaters, we shall not
   shortly have a rasher on the coals for money.

g) My daughter!—O my ducats!—O my daughter! Fled with a Christian!—O my Christian
   ducats! Justice! the law! my ducats, and my
   daughter!

                    ERNEST REDEKOP, M.A.
                    Trinity College, Toronto

THE MERCHANT
OF VENICE

DRAMATIS PERSONAE

DUKE OF VENICE.

PRINCE OF MOROCCO, ⎫
PRINCE OF ARRAGON, ⎭ *suitors to Portia.*

ANTONIO, *a merchant of Venice.*

BASSANIO, *his kinsman and friend.*

SOLANIO, ⎫
SALARINO, ⎬ *friends to Antonio and Bassanio.*
GRATIANO, ⎭

LORENZO, *in love with Jessica.*

SHYLOCK, *a rich Jew.*

TUBAL, *a Jew, his friend.*

LAUNCELOT GOBBO, *a clown, servant to Shylock.*

OLD GOBBO, *father to Launcelot.*

LEONARDO, *servant to Bassanio.*

BALTHAZAR, ⎫
STEPHANO, ⎭ *servants to Portia.*

PORTIA, *a rich heiress.*

NERISSA, *her waiting-maid.*

JESSICA, *daughter to Shylock.*

MAGNIFICOES OF VENICE, OFFICERS OF THE COURT OF JUSTICE, GAOLER, SERVANTS, *and other* ATTENDANTS.

SCENE—*Partly at Venice, and partly at Belmont, the seat of Portia, on the Continent.*

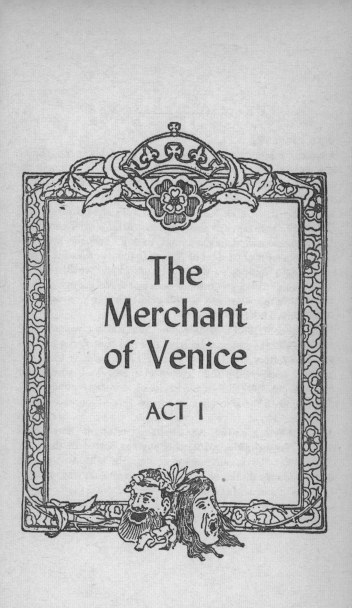

The Merchant of Venice

ACT I

ACT I

ANTONIO, a merchant of Venice, and two of his friends, Salarino and Solanio, are conversing. The two friends comment on Antonio's melancholy, thinking that he fears for the safety of his ships. He replies that this is not the cause of his sadness. They meet three other Venetians: Bassanio, the dearest friend of Antonio, and Lorenzo and Gratiano. After a brief conversation, all leave except Bassanio and Antonio. Bassanio, who has already spent a great deal of Antonio's money, asks his friend for more, so that he can woo the beautiful and wealthy Portia of Belmont. Although Antonio does not have enough money at hand, he tells Bassanio he will gladly let him use his credit with moneylenders in Venice.

At Belmont, Portia and Nerissa, her waiting woman, discuss the various suitors who have been wooing Portia according to a lottery devised by Portia's father: she is to marry whoever chooses the right casket of three, gold, silver, and lead. As four suitors leave, the Prince of Morocco is announced.

In Venice, Bassanio tries to borrow three thousand ducats from Shylock, a Jewish moneylender, whom he invites to dinner. Shylock refuses the invitation. Antonio enters and Shylock, in an aside, reveals his envious hatred of the merchant, who "lends out money gratis." He tells Antonio the reasons for his dislike of him, then hypocritically says he will lend the money without interest if Antonio, "in a merry sport," will promise to let him cut off a pound of his flesh if the bond is forfeited. Despite Bassanio's misgivings, Antonio signs the bond.

ACT I. Scene I.

Venice. A street.

Enter ANTONIO, SALARINO, *and* SOLANIO.

ANTONIO.

In sooth[1] I know not why I am so sad:
It wearies me; you say it wearies you;
But how I caught it, found it, or came by it,
What stuff 'tis made of, whereof it is born,
I am to learn;
And such a want-wit sadness makes of me,
That I have much ado to know myself.

SALARINO.

Your mind is tossing on the ocean;
There, where your argosies[2] with portly sail,—
Like signiors and rich burghers of the flood,
Or, as it were, the pageants of the sea,—
Do overpeer the petty traffickers,
That curtsey to them, do them reverence,
As they fly by them with their woven wings.

SOLANIO.

Believe me, sir, had I such venture forth,
The better part of my affections would
Be with my hopes abroad. I should be still
Plucking the grass, to know where sits the wind;
Peering in maps for ports, and piers, and roads;
And every object that might make me fear

---

[1] in sooth: in fact; in truth.
[2] argosies: merchant ships.

3

Misfortune to my ventures, out of doubt
Would make me sad.

SALARINO.

                My wind, cooling my broth.
Would blow me to an ague[1] when I thought
What harm a wind too great might do at sea.
I should not see the sandy hour-glass run,
But I should think of shallows and of flats;
And see my wealthy Andrew[2] dockt in sand,
Vailing[3] her high-top lower than her ribs,
To kiss her burial. Should I go to church,
And see the holy edifice of stone,
And not bethink me straight of dangerous rocks,
Which touching but my gentle vessel's side,
Would scatter all her spices on the stream;
Enrobe the roaring waters with my silks;
And, in a word, but even now worth this,
And now worth nothing? Shall I have the thought
To think on this; and shall I lack the thought,
That such a thing bechanced would make me sad?
But tell not me; I know Antonio
Is sad to think upon his merchandise.

ANTONIO.

Believe me, no: I thank my fortune for it,
My ventures are not in one bottom[4] trusted,
Nor to one place; nor is my whole estate
Upon the fortune of this present year;
Therefore my merchandise makes me not sad.

SOLANIO.

Why, then you are in love.

ANTONIO.

                Fie, fie!

---

[1] **ague**: chill.
[2] **Andrew**: name of his ship.
[3] **vailing**: to lower or bow as in surrender.
[4] **bottom**: ship or hold of a ship.

SALARINO.

Not in love neither? Then let's say you're sad,
Because you are not merry: and 'twere as easy
For you to laugh, and leap, and say you are merry,
Because you are not sad. Now, by two-headed Janus,[1]
Nature hath framed strange fellows in her time:
Some that will evermore peep through[2] their eyes,
And laugh, like parrots, at a bag-piper;[2]
And other of such vinegar aspect,
That they'll not show their teeth in way of smile,
Though Nestor[3] swear that jest be laughable.

SOLANIO.

Here comes Bassanio, your most noble kinsman,
Gratiano, and Lorenzo. Fare ye well:
We leave you now with better company.

SALARINO.

I would have stay'd till I had made you merry,
If worthier friends had not prevented me.

ANTONIO.

Your worth is very dear in my regard.
I take it, your own business calls on you,
And you embrace th' occasion to depart.

Enter BASSANIO, LORENZO, *and* GRATIANO.

SALARINO.

Good morrow, my good lords.

BASSANIO.

Good signiors both, when shall we laugh? say, when?
You grow exceeding strange: must it be so?

SALARINO.

We'll make our leisures to attend on yours.[4]

                              [*Exeunt* SALARINO *and* SOLANIO.

---

[1] **Janus**: the porter of heaven in Roman mythology; always represented with two heads. [2] **And laugh, like parrots, at a bag-piper**: laugh at something that is not funny; the dirge-like music of a bagpipe was considered cheerful only by the Scots. [3] **Nestor**: the oldest and wisest of the Greek chiefs in the Trojan War. [4] **We'll make our leisures to attend on yours**: we shall make ourselves available when you are free.

LORENZO.

My Lord Bassanio, since you have found Antonio,
We two will leave you: but, at dinner-time,
I pray you, have in mind where we must meet.

BASSANIO.

I will not fail you.

GRATIANO.

You look not well, Signior Antonio;
You have too much respect upon the world:[1]
They lose it that do buy it with much care:
Believe me, you are marvellously changed.

ANTONIO.

I hold [2] the world but as the world, Gratiano;
A stage, where every man must play a part,
And mine a sad one.

GRATIANO.

            Let me play the fool:
With mirth and laughter let old wrinkles come;
And let my liver rather heat with wine
Than my heart cool with mortifying groans.
Why should a man, whose blood is warm within,
Sit like his grandsire cut in alabaster? [3]
Sleep when he wakes? and creep into the jaundice
By being peevish? I tell thee what, Antonio,—
I love thee, and it is my love that speaks,—
There are a sort of men, whose visages
Do cream and mantle like a standing pond;[4]
And do a wilful stillness entertain,[5]
With purpose to be drest in an opinion[6]
Of wisdom, gravity, profound conceit;
As who should say, 'I am Sir Oracle,[7]

---

[1] respect upon the world: regard for worldly matters. [2] hold: regard. [3] alabaster: a hard, translucent stone, usually white; in this case, a tombstone. [4] cream and mantle like a standing pond: scum over like a stagnant pond. [5] entertain: maintain. [6] an opinion: a reputation. [7] Sir Oracle: the wise one who knows everything.

And when I ope[1] my lips, let no dog barkl'
O my Antonio, I do know of these,
That therefore only are reputed wise
For saying nothing; when, I am very sure,
If they should speak, would almost damn those ears,
Which, hearing them, would call their brothers fools.
I'll tell thee more of this another time:
But fish not, with this melancholy bait,
For this fool-gudgeon,[2] this opinion.—
Come, good Lorenzo.—Fare ye well awhile:
I'll end my exhortation after dinner.

LORENZO.

Well, we will leave you, then, till dinner-time:
I must be one of these same dumb wise men,
For Gratiano never lets me speak.

GRATIANO.

Well, keep me company but two years moe,[3]
Thou shalt not know the sound of thine own tongue.

ANTONIO.

Farewell: I'll grow a talker for this gear.[4]

GRATIANO.

Thanks, i'faith, for silence is only a commendable
In a neat's tongue[5] dried, and a maid not vendible.[6]

[*Exeunt* GRATIANO *and* LORENZO.

ANTONIO.

Is that any thing now?

BASSANIO.

Gratiano speaks an infinite deal of nothing, more than any
man in all Venice. His reasons are as two grains of wheat

---

[1] ope: open.
[2] gudgeon: a small fish, easily caught and often used for bait.
[3] moe: more.
[4] gear: stuff; nonsense.
[5] neat's tongue: cow's tongue.
[6] vendible: salable; marriageable.

hid in two bushels of chaff: you shall seek all day ere you
find them; and when you have them, they are not worth the
search.

ANTONIO.

Well; tell me now, what lady is the same
To whom you swore a secret pilgrimage,
That you to-day promised to tell me of?

BASSANIO.

'Tis not unknown to you, Antonio,
How much I have disabled mine estate,[1]
By something showing a more swelling port[2]
Than my faint means would grant continuance:
Nor do I now make moan to be abridged [3]
From such a noble rate; but my chief care
Is, to come fairly off from the great debts,
Wherein my time, something too prodigal,
Hath left me gaged.[4] To you, Antonio,
I owe the most, in money and in love;
And from your love I have a warranty
To unburden all my plots and purposes
How to get clear of all the debts I owe.

ANTONIO.

I pray you, good Bassanio, let me know it;
And if it stand, as you yourself still do,
Within the eye of honour, be assured
My purse, my person, my extremest means,
Lie all unlockt to your occasions.[5]

BASSANIO.

In my school-days, when I had lost one shaft,
I shot his fellow of the selfsame flight
The selfsame way with more advised watch,[6]
To find the other forth; and by advent'ring[7] both,

---

[1] **disabled mine estate:** reduced my fortune. [2] **swelling port:** high
style of living. [3] **abridged:** cut down. [4] **gaged:** pledged; mortgaged.
[5] **occasions:** needs. [6] **advised watch:** careful attention. [7] **advent'ring:**
risking.

I oft found both: I urge this childhood proof,
Because what follows is pure innocence.[1]
I owe you much; and, like a wilful youth,
That which I owe is lost: but if you please
To shoot another arrow that self way
Which you did shoot the first, I do not doubt,
As I will watch the aim, or to find both,
Or bring your latter hazard back again,
And thankfully rest[2] debtor for the first.

ANTONIO.

You know me well; and herein spend but time
To wind about my love with circumstance;[3]
And out of doubt you do me now more wrong
In making question of my uttermost,[4]
Than if you had made waste of all I have:
Then do but say to me what I should do,
That in your knowledge may by me be done,
And I am prest unto it: therefore, speak.

BASSANIO.

In Belmont is a lady richly left;[5]
And she is fair, and, fairer than that word,
Of wondrous virtues: sometimes from her eyes
I did receive fair speechless messages:
Her name is Portia; nothing undervalued
To Cato's daughter, Brutus' Portia:
Nor is the wide world ignorant of her worth;
For the four winds blow in from every coast
Renowned suitors: and her sunny locks
Hang on her temples like a golden fleece;
Which makes her seat of Belmont Colchos' strond,[6]
And many Jasons come in quest of her.
O my Antonio, had I but the means

---

[1] pure innocence: naïveté; folly. [2] rest: remain. [3] circumstance: formality. [4] making question of my uttermost: questioning the extent of my willingness. [5] richly left: of inherited wealth. [6] Colchos' strond: the shore of Colchos; here Jason came in search of the Golden Fleece.

To hold a rival place with one of them,
I have a mind presages me such thrift,
That I should questionless be fortunate! [1]

ANTONIO

Thou know'st that all my fortunes are at sea;
Neither have I money, nor commodity
To raise a present[2] sum: therefore, go forth;
Try what my credit can in Venice do:
That shall be rackt,[3] even to the uttermost,
To furnish thee to Belmont, to fair Portia.
Go, presently inquire, and so will I,
Where money is; and I no question make,
To have it of my trust,[4] or for my sake.   [*Exeunt.*

SCENE II.

Belmont. A room in PORTIA'S *house.*

Enter PORTIA *and* NERISSA.

PORTIA.

By my troth, Nerissa, my little body is aweary of this great
world.

NERISSA.

You would be, sweet madam, if your miseries were in the
same abundance as your good fortunes are: and yet, for aught
I see, they are as sick that surfeit with too much, as they that
starve with nothing It is no mean happiness, therefore, to be
seated in the mean:[5] superfluity comes sooner by white hairs;
but competency[6] lives longer.

PORTIA.

Good sentences,[7] and well pronounced.

---

[1] **I have a mind presages me such thrift,/ That I should questionless be fortunate:** I have such a premonition of success that I
shall undoubtedly become rich. [2] **a present:** an immediate. [3] **rackt:**
stretched as upon a rack; extended. [4] **of my trust:** through con-
fidence in my ability [5] **in the mean:** to have neither too much nor
too little. [6] **competency:** adequate wealth. [7] **Good sentences:** good
maxims.

NERISSA.

They would be better, if well follow'd.

PORTIA.

If to do were as easy as to know what were good to do, chapels had been churches, and poor men's cottages princes' palaces. It is a good divine[1] that follows his own instructions: I can easier teach twenty what were good to be done, than be one of the twenty to follow mine own teaching. The brain may devise laws for the blood;[2] but a hot temper leaps o'er a cold decree: such a hare is madness the youth, to skip o'er the meshes[3] of good-counsel the cripple. But this reasoning is not in the fashion to choose me a husband:—O me, the word 'choose'! I may neither choose who I would, nor refuse who I dislike; so is the will of a living daughter curb'd by the will of a dead father.—Is it not hard, Nerissa, that I cannot choose one, nor refuse none?

NERISSA.

Your father was ever virtuous; and holy men, at their death, have good inspirations: therefore, the lottery, that he hath devised in these three chests of gold, silver, and lead,— whereof who chooses his meaning chooses you,—will, no doubt, never be chosen by any rightly, but one who shall rightly love. But what warmth is there in your affection towards any of these princely suitors that are already come?

PORTIA.

I pray thee, over-name them; and as thou namest them, I will

---

[1] **good divine:** good clergyman or counselor.
[2] **blood:** impulses; passions.
[3] **meshes:** the meshes of the net that would restrain (netting of rabbits or hares).

describe them; and, according to my description, level at my affection.[1]

NERISSA.

First, there is the Neapolitan prince.

PORTIA.

Ay, that's a colt indeed, for he doth nothing but talk of his horse; and he makes it a great appropriation[2] to his own good parts, that he can shoe him himself. I am much afeard my lady his mother play'd false with a smith.

NERISSA.

Then there is the County[3] Palatine.

PORTIA.

He doth nothing but frown; as who should say, 'An[4] you will not have me, choose:' he hears merry tales, and smiles not: I fear he will prove the weeping philosopher[5] when he grows old, being so full of unmannerly sadness in his youth. I had rather be married to a Death's-head with a bone in his mouth than to either of these:—God defend me from these two!

NERISSA.

How say you by the French lord, Monsieur Le Bon?

PORTIA.

God made him, and therefore let him pass for a man. In truth, I know it is a sin to be a mocker: but, he!—why, he hath a horse better than the Neapolitan's; a better bad habit of frowning than the Count Palatine: he is every man in no man;[6] if a throstle[7] sing, he falls straight[8] a-capering;[9] he will fence with his own shadow: if I should marry him, I

---

[1] level at my affection: guess my feelings toward them. [2] appropriation: asset; literally, "attribution." [3] County: Count. [4] An: if. [5] weeping philosopher: an allusion to Heraclitus of Ephesus. [6] every man in no man: i.e., too mercurial; changeable. [7] throstle: thrush. [8] straight: at once. [9] a-capering: to dancing.

should marry twenty husbands. If he would despise me,
I would forgive him; for if he love me to madness, I shall
never requite him.

NERISSA.

What say you, then, to Falconbridge, the young baron of
England?

PORTIA.

You know I say nothing to him: for he understands not me,
nor I him: he hath neither Latin, French, nor Italian; and
you will come into the court and swear that I have a poor
pennyworth in the English. He is a proper[1] man's picture;
but, alas, who can converse with a dumb-show?[2] How oddly
he is suited![3] I think he bought his doublet in Italy, his
round hose in France, his bonnet in Germany, and his behaviour every where.

NERISSA.

What think you of the Scottish lord, his neighbour?

PORTIA.

That he hath a neighbourly charity in him; for he borrow'd
a box of the ear of the Englishman,[4] and swore he would
pay him again when he was able: I think the Frenchman
became his surety, and seal'd under for another.[5]

NERISSA.

How like you the young German, the Duke of Saxony's
nephew?

PORTIA.

Very vilely in the morning, when he is sober; and most vilely
in the afternoon, when he is drunk: when he is best, he is a
little worse than a man; and when he is worst, he is little
better than a beast. An the worst fall that ever fell, I hope

---

[1] proper: handsome.
[2] dumb-show: pantomime.
[3] suited: dressed.
[4] borrow'd/a box of the ear of the Englishman: received a blow
from the Englishman without retaliating.
[5] seal'd under for another: put his seal under the Scot's on the bond.

I shall make shift to go without him.

NERISSA.

If he should offer to choose, and choose the right casket, you should refuse to perform your father's will, if you should refuse to accept him.

PORTIA.

Therefore, for fear of the worst, I pray thee, set a deep glass of Rhenish wine on the contrary casket; for, if the devil be within, and that temptation without, I know he will choose it. I will do anything, Nerissa, ere I will be married to a sponge.[1]

NERISSA.

You need not fear, lady, the having any of these lords: they have acquainted me with their determinations; which is, indeed, to return to their home, and to trouble you with no more suit, unless you may be won by some other sort[2] than your father's imposition, depending on the caskets.

PORTIA.

If I live to be as old as Sibylla,[3] I will die as chaste as Diana,[4] unless I be obtain'd by the manner of my father's will. I am glad this parcel of wooers are so reasonable; for there is not one among them but I dote on his very absence; and I pray God grant them a fair departure.

NERISSA.

Do you not remember, lady, in your father's time, a Venetian, a scholar and a soldier, that came hither in company of the Marquis of Montferrat?

---

[1] sponge: drunkard.
[2] by some other sort: in some other manner.
[3] Sibylla: the Cumaean Sibyl (of whom Ovid and Vergil wrote), whose life was protracted to 1,000 years.
[4] Diana: the virgin goddess of the hunt.

PORTIA.

Yes, yes, it was Bassanio: as I think, so was he call'd.

NERISSA.

True, madam: he, of all the men that ever my foolish eyes lookt upon, was the best deserving a fair lady.

PORTIA.

I remember him well; and I remember him worthy of thy praise.

Enter a SERVANT.

How now! what news?

SERVANT.

The four strangers seek for you, madam, to take their leave: and there is a forerunner come from a fifth, the Prince of Morocco; who brings word, the prince his master will be here to-night.

PORTIA.

If I could bid the fifth welcome with so good a heart as I can bid the other four farewell, I should be glad of his approach: if he have the condition[1] of a saint and the complexion[2] of a devil, I had rather he should shrive me[3] than wive me.

Come, Nerissa.—Sirrah, go before.—

Whiles we shut the gates upon one wooer, another knocks at the door.   [*Exeunt.*

---

[1] condition: character.
[2] complexion: appearance.
[3] shrive me: give me absolution for my sins.

SCENE III.

Venice. A public place.

Enter BASSANIO *with* SHYLOCK *the Jew.*

SHYLOCK.

Three thousand ducats,[1]—well.

BASSANIO.

Ay, sir, for three months.

SHYLOCK.

For three months,—well.

BASSANIO.

For the which, as I told you, Antonio shall be bound.[2]

SHYLOCK.

Antonio shall become bound,—well.

BASSANIO.

May you stead [3] me? will you pleasure me? shall I know your answer?

SHYLOCK.

Three thousand ducats for three months, and Antonio bound.

BASSANIO.

Your answer to that.

SHYLOCK.

Antonio is a good man.

BASSANIO.

Have you heard any imputation to the contrary?

SHYLOCK.

Ho, no, no, no, no;—my meaning, in saying he is a good man is to have you understand me that he is sufficient. Yet his means are in supposition:[4] he hath an argosy bound to Tripolis, another to the Indies; I understand, moreover, upon

---

[1] **ducats:** gold coins.
[2] **bound:** under bond.
[3] **stead:** help.
[4] **are in supposition:** are not certain.

the Rialto,[1] he hath a third at Mexico, a fourth for England,
—and other ventures he hath, squander'd[2] abroad. But ships
are but boards, sailors but men: there be land-rats and water-
rats, water-thieves and land-thieves, I mean pirates; and then
there is the peril of waters, winds, and rocks. The man is,
notwithstanding, sufficient:—three thousand ducats.—I think
I may take his bond.

BASSANIO.
Be assured you may.

SHYLOCK.
I will be assured I may; and, that I may be assured, I will
bethink me. May I speak with Antonio?

BASSANIO.
If it please you to dine with us.

SHYLOCK.
Yes, to smell pork; to eat of the habitation which your
prophet the Nazarite[3] conjured the devil into. I will buy with
you, sell with you, talk with you, walk with you, and so following; but I will not eat with you, drink with you, nor pray
with you. What news on the Rialto?—Who is he comes here?

Enter ANTONIO.

BASSANIO.
This is Signior Antonio.

SHYLOCK [*aside*].
How like a fawning publican[4] he looks!
I hate him for he is a Christian!

---

[1] Rialto: a famous street and bridge in Venice (the Venetian Exchange).
[2] squander'd: scattered.
[3] the Nazarite: Christ.
[4] publican: innkeeper.

But more, for that, in low simplicity,[1]
He lends out money gratis, and brings down
The rate of usance[2] here with us in Venice.
If I can catch him once upon the hip,[3]
I will feed fat the ancient grudge I bear him.
He hates our sacred nation;[4] and he rails,
Even there where merchants most do congregate,
On me, my bargains, and my well-won thrift,[5]
Which he calls interest. Cursed be my tribe,
If I forgive him!

    BASSANIO.
                Shylock, do you hear?

    SHYLOCK.
I am debating of my present store;
And, by the near guess of my memory,
I cannot instantly raise up the gross
Of full three thousand ducats. What of that?
Tubal, a wealthy Hebrew of my tribe,
Will furnish me. But soft! how many months
Do you desire?—Rest you fair, good signior;   [*to* ANTONIO.
Your worship was the last man in our mouths.

    ANTONIO.
Shylock, although I neither lend nor borrow
By taking nor by giving of excess,
Yet, to supply the ripe wants[6] of my friend,
I'll break a custom.—Is he yet possest[7]
How much ye would?

    SHYLOCK.
            Ay, ay, three thousand ducats.

---

[1] **in low simplicity:** in humble ignorance. [2] **usance:** interest. [3] **catch him one upon the hip:** use the hip as a fulcrum to throw him (a wrestling term). [4] **sacred nation:** the Jews. [5] **thrift:** riches. [6] **ripe wants:** urgent needs. [7] **Is he yet possest:** has he been told.

ANTONIO.

And for three months.

SHYLOCK.

I had forgot,—three months, you told me so.
Well, then, your bond; and let me see,—but hear you;
Methought you said you neither lend nor borrow
Upon advantage.

ANTONIO.

I do never use it.

SHYLOCK.

When Jacob grazed his uncle Laban's sheep,[1]—
This Jacob from our holy Abram[2] was
(As his wise mother wrought in his behalf)
The third possessor; ay, he was the third,—

ANTONIO.

And what of him? did he take interest?

SHYLOCK.

No, not take interest; not as you would say,
Directly interest: mark what Jacob did.
When Laban and himself were compromised [3]
That all the eanlings[4] which were streakt and pied [5]
Should fall as Jacob's hire, the ewes, being rank,
In th' end of autumn turned to the rams;
And when the work of generation was
Between these woolly breeders in the act,
The skilful shepherd peel'd me certain wands,
And, in the doing of the deed of kind,
He stuck them up before the fulsome ewes,
Who, then conceiving, did in eaning time[6]
Fall [7] parti-colour'd lambs, and those were Jacob's.
This was a way to thrive, and he was blest:
And thrift is blessing, if men steal it not.

---

[1] When Jacob grazed his uncle Laban's sheep: Shylock tries to defend himself by citing an example from the Bible. [2] Abram: Abraham. [3] compromised: agreed. [4] eanlings: new-born lambs; yearlings. [5] pied: spotted. [6] eaning time: lambing time. [7] Fall: give birth to.

ANTONIO.

This was a venture, sir, that Jacob served for;
A thing not in his power to bring to pass,
But sway'd and fashion'd by the hand of heaven.
Was this inserted to make interest good? [1]
Or is your gold and silver ewes and rams?

SHYLOCK.

I cannot tell: I make it breed as fast:—
But note me, signior.

ANTONIO.

              Mark you this, Bassanio,
The devil can cite Scripture for his purpose.
An evil soul, producing holy witness,
Is like a villain with a smiling cheek;
A goodly apple rotten at the heart:
O, what a goodly outside falsehood hath!

SHYLOCK.

Three thousand ducats,—'tis a good round sum.
Three months from twelve,—then, let me see, the rate—

ANTONIO.

Well, Shylock, shall we be beholden to you?

SHYLOCK.

Signior Antonio, many a time and oft,
In the Rialto, you have rated [2] me
About my moneys and my usances:
Still have I borne it with a patient shrug;
For sufferance is the badge of all our tribe:
You call me misbeliever, cut-throat dog,
And spit upon my Jewish gaberdine, [3]
And all for use of that which is mine own.
Well, then, it now appears you need my help:

---

[1] make interest good: justify charging interest.
[2] rated: berated.
[3] gaberdine: loose cloak or mantle.

Go to, then;[1] you come to me, and you say,
'Shylock, we would have moneys:'—you say so;
You, that did void your rheum[2] upon my beard,
And foot[3] me as you spurn a stranger cur
Over your threshold: moneys is your suit.
What should I say to you? Should I not say,
'Hath a dog money? is it possible
A cur can lend three thousand ducats?' or
Shall I bend low, and in a bondman's key,[4]
With bated breath and whispering humbleness,
Say this,—
'Fair sir, you spit on me on Wednesday last;
You spurn'd me such a day; another time
You call'd me dog; and for these courtesies
I'll lend you thus much moneys'?

ANTONIO.

I am as like to call thee so again,
To spit on thee again, to spurn thee too.
If thou wilt lend this money, lend it not
As to thy friends—for when did friendship take
A breed[5] for barren metal of his friend?—
But lend it rather to thine enemy;
Who if he break,[6] thou mayst with better face
Exact the penalty.

SHYLOCK.

Why, look you, how you storm!
I would be friends with you, and have your love,
Forget the shames that you have stain'd me with,
Supply your present wants, and take no doit[7]
Of usance for my moneys,
And you'll not hear me: this is kind I offer.

---

[1] Go to, then: very well, then. [2] void your rheum: spit. [3] foot: kick.
[4] bondman's key: humble voice. [5] breed: Aristotle claimed that since
it would be unnatural for gold and silver, which are barren, to
have offspring, it was also unnatural to charge interest on them;
hence, breed—unnatural offspring. [6] break: goes bankrupt. [7] doit:
a coin of low value; a fraction of a farthing.

BASSANIO.

This were kindness.

SHYLOCK.

This kindness will I show:—
Go with me to a notary, seal me there
Your single bond;[1] and, in a merry sport,[2]
If you repay me not on such a day,
In such a place, such sum or sums as are
Exprest in the condition, let the forfeit
Be nominated for an equal [3] pound
Of your fair flesh, to be cut off and taken
In what part of your body pleaseth me.

ANTONIO.

Content,[4] i'faith: I'll seal to such a bond,
And say there is much kindness in the Jew.

BASSANIO.

You shall not seal to such a bond for me:
I'll rather dwell in my necessity.

ANTONIO.

Why, fear not, man; I will not forfeit it:
Within these two months, that's a month before
This bond expires, I do expect return
Of thrice three times the value of this bond.

SHYLOCK.

O father Abram, what these Christians are,
Whose own hard dealings teaches them suspect
The thoughts of others!—Pray you, tell me this;
If he should break his day, what should I gain
By the exaction of the forfeiture?
A pound of man's flesh taken from a man
Is not so estimable, profitable neither,
As flesh of muttons,[5] beefs, or goats. I say,

---

[1] single bond: bond without security.
[2] merry sport: spirit of fun.
[3] equal: exact.
[4] Content: agreed.
[5] muttons: sheep.

To buy his favour, I extend this friendship:
If he will take it, so; if not, adieu;
And, for my love, I pray you wrong me not.

    ANTONIO.

Yes, Shylock, I will seal unto this bond.

    SHYLOCK.

Then meet me forthwith at the notary's,—
Give him direction for this merry bond;
And I will go and purse the ducats straight;
See to my house, left in the fearful [1] guard
Of an unthrifty knave;[2] and presently
I will be with you.

    ANTONIO.

              Hie thee, gentle Jew.

                          [*Exit* SHYLOCK.

The Hebrew will turn Christian: he grows kind.

    BASSANIO.

I like not fair terms and a villain's mind.

    ANTONIO.

Come on: in this there can be no dismay;
My ships come home a month before the day.   [*Exeunt.*

---

[1] fearful: dangerous; untrustworthy.
[2] knave: servant (used contemptuously).

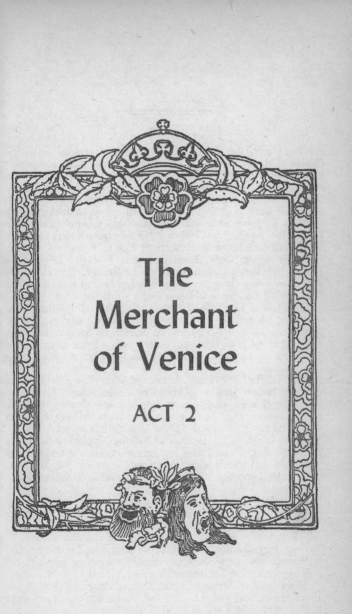

The
Merchant
of Venice

ACT 2

ACT II

At Belmont, the Prince of Morocco prepares to make his choice of the three caskets. In Venice, meanwhile, Launcelot Gobbo, servant of Shylock, debates with himself whether or not to leave the service of the Jew. He meets his old half-blind father and tells him he is leaving Shylock's service. They meet Bassanio, and Old Gobbo, with many confusing interruptions by Launcelot, asks that Bassanio accept his son into his service. As the two Gobbos leave, Gratiano enters and asks Bassanio's permission to accompany him to Belmont.

In the Jew's house, Launcelot bids a tearful farewell to Jessica, Shylock's daughter. After he leaves, she expresses shame at being daughter to such a father and looks forward to marrying Lorenzo and becoming a Christian.

Meanwhile, Gratiano, Lorenzo, Salarino, and Solanio are planning their parts in a masque which is to take place at Bassanio's dinner for Shylock. Launcelot, on his way to invite Shylock to eat with Bassanio, enters with a letter from Jessica for Lorenzo, in which she describes her plan to elope with him.

Shylock, hearing from Launcelot that there will be a masque, orders Jessica to keep the house closed. Launcelot slily tells Jessica that Lorenzo will come shortly. Shylock leaves, saying that he hopes Launcelot will help Bassanio waste the three thousand ducats Antonio has borrowed.

Later, Lorenzo, Gratiano, and Salarino appear at Shylock's house. Jessica, dressed as a boy, gives Lorenzo a casket filled with gold and jewels and goes off with him and Salarino. Antonio enters and tells Gratiano that Bassanio is expected immediately.

At Belmont, the Prince of Morocco, reasoning that only gold is a fit setting for such a gem as Portia, receives a death's-head as reward.

Salarino and Solanio, meanwhile, describe the passion of Shylock when he discovered that his daughter, his ducats, and his jewels were gone. Salarino mentions news of losses at sea and expresses fear for Antonio's safety.

The Prince of Arragon, next suitor at Belmont, chooses the silver casket, and gets a fool's head. As he leaves, a messenger enters, announcing the arrival of Bassanio.

ACT II. Scene I.

Belmont. A room in PORTIA's *house.*

Enter the PRINCE OF MOROCCO, *a tawny Moor all in white, and three or four* FOLLOWERS *accordingly, with* PORTIA, NERISSA, *and their* TRAIN. *Flourish of cornets.*

PRINCE OF MOROCCO.
Mislike me not for my complexion,
The shadow'd livery of the burnisht sun,[1]
To whom I am a neighbour and near bred.
Bring me the fairest creature northward born,
Where Phœbus'[2] fire scarce thaws the icicles,
And let us make incision for your love,
To prove whose blood is reddest, his or mine.
I tell thee, lady, this aspect of mine
Hath fear'd[3] the valiant: by my love, I swear
The best-regarded virgins of our clime
Hath loved it too: I would not change this hue,
Except to steal your thoughts, my gentle queen.
PORTIA.
In terms of choice[4] I am not solely led
By nice direction[5] of a maiden's eyes;
Besides, the lottery of my destiny
Bars me the right of voluntary choosing:
But, if my father had not scanted[6] me,
And hedg'd me by his will, to yield myself
His wife who wins me by that means I told you,
Yourself, renowned prince, then stood as fair
As any comer I have lookt on yet
For my affection.
PRINCE OF MOROCCO.
                    Even for that I thank you:

---

[1] **The shadow'd livery of the burnisht sun:** his dark skin shows that he comes from a sunny climate, just as the livery of a servant shows to what lord he belongs. [2] **Phœbus:** Phœbus Apollo, god of the sun. [3] **fear'd:** frightened. [4] **In terms of choice:** in making my choice. [5] **nice direction:** foolish or flighty command. [6] **scanted:** stinted; limited.

27

Therefore, I pray you, lead me to the caskets,
To try my fortune. By this scimitar,[1]
That slew the Sophy[2] and a Persian prince
That won three fields of Sultan Solyman,[3]
I would outstare the sternest eyes that look,
Outbrave the heart most daring on the earth,
Pluck the young sucking-cubs from the she-bear.
Yea, mock the lion when he roars for prey,
To win thee, lady. But, alas the while!
If Hercules and Lichas[4] play at dice
Which is the better man, the greater throw
May turn by fortune from the weaker hand:
So is Alcides[5] beaten by his page;
And so may I, blind Fortune leading me,
Miss that which one unworthier may attain,
And die with grieving.

    PORTIA.

                You must take your chance
And either not attempt to choose at all,
Or swear before you choose,—if you choose wrong,
Never to speak to lady afterward
In way of marriage: therefore be advised.[6]

    PRINCE OF MOROCCO.

Nor will not. Come, bring me unto my chance.

    PORTIA.

First, forward to the temple: after dinner
Your hazard shall be made.

    PRINCE OF MOROCCO.

                Good fortune, then!
To make me blest or cursed'st among men.

                    [Cornets, and exeunt.

---

[1] scimitar: curved sword.
[2] Sophy: former title of King of Persia (Iran).
[3] Sultan Solyman: the Sultan of Turkey.
[4] Lichas: attendant and friend of Hercules.
[5] Alcides: Hercules.
[6] be advised: consider carefully.

Scene II.

Venice. A street.

Enter LAUNCELOT *the Clown, alone.*

LAUNCELOT GOBBO.

Certainly my conscience will serve me to run from this Jew my master. The fiend is at mine elbow, and tempts me, saying to me, 'Gobbo, Launcelot Gobbo, good Launcelot,' or 'good Gobbo,' or 'good Launcelot Gobbo, use your legs, take the start, run away.' My conscience says, 'No; take heed, honest Launcelot; take heed, honest Gobbo,' or, as aforesaid, 'honest Launcelot Gobbo; do not run; scorn running with thy heels.' Well, the most courageous fiend bids me pack:[1] '*Via!*' says the fiend, 'away!' says the fiend; 'for the heavens,[2] rouse up a brave mind,' says the fiend, 'and run.' Well, my conscience, hanging about the neck of my heart, says very wisely to me, 'My honest friend Launcelot, being an honest man's son,'— or rather an honest woman's son;—for, indeed, my father did something smack,[3] something grow to,—he had a kind of taste;—well, my conscience says, 'Launcelot, budge not.' 'Budge,' says the fiend. 'Budge not,' says my conscience. 'Conscience,' say I, 'you counsel well; 'fiend,' say I, 'you counsel well:' to be ruled by my conscience, I should stay with the Jew my master, who—God bless the mark!—is a kind of devil; and, to run away from the Jew, I should be ruled by the fiend, who, saving your reverence, is the devil himself. Certainly the Jew is the very devil incarnal;[4] and, in my conscience,[5] my conscience is but a kind of hard con-

---

[1] pack: be off.
[2] for the heavens: for heaven's sake.
[3] did/something smack: was a little inclined toward dishonesty.
[4] incarnal: incarnate (in the flesh).
[5] in/my conscience: as I see it.

science, to offer to counsel me to stay with the Jew. The fiend
gives the more friendly counsel: I will run, fiend; my heels
are at your command; I will run.

Enter OLD GOBBO, *with a basket.*

OLD GOBBO.

Master young man, you, I pray you, which is the way to
master Jew's?

LAUNCELOT GOBBO [*aside*].

O heavens, this is my true-begotten father! who, being more
than sand-blind,[1] high-gravel-blind, knows me not:—I will try
confusions with him.

OLD GOBBO.

Master young gentleman, I pray you, which is the way to
master Jew's?

LAUNCELOT GOBBO.

Turn up on your right hand at the next turning, but, at the
next turning of all, on your left; marry,[2] at the very next turning, turn of no hand, but turn down indirectly to the Jew's
house.

OLD GOBBO.

By God's sonties,[3] 'twill be a hard way to hit. Can you tell
me whether one Launcelot, that dwells with him, dwell with
him or no?

LAUNCELOT GOBBO.

Talk you of young Master Launcelot?—[*aside*] Mark me
now; now will I raise the waters.[4]—Talk you of young Master
Launcelot?

OLD GOBBO.

No master, sir, but a poor man's son: his father, though I say
it, is an honest exceeding poor man, and, God be thankt, well
to live.

---

[1] sand-blind: half-blind; dim-sighted (a corruption of *samblind*).
[2] marry: by the Virgin Mary.
[3] God's sonties: a popular oath of the times without any clear
meaning.
[4] raise the waters: bring tears to his eyes.

LAUNCELOT GOBBO.

Well, let his father be what a' will, we talk of young Master Launcelot.

OLD GOBBO.

Your worship's friend, and Launcelot, sir.

LAUNCELOT GOBBO.

But, I pray you, *ergo*, old man, *ergo*,[1] I beseech you, talk you of young Master Launcelot?

OLD GOBBO.

Of Launcelot, an't please your mastership.

LAUNCELOT GOBBO.

Ergo, Master Launcelot. Talk not of Master Launcelot, father; for the young gentleman—according to Fates and Destinies, and such odd sayings, the Sisters Three,[2] and such branches of learning—is, indeed, deceased; or, as you would say in plain terms, gone to heaven.

OLD GOBBO.

Marry, God forbid! the boy was the very staff of my age, my very prop.

LAUNCELOT GOBBO.

Do I look like a cudgel or a hovel-post, a staff, or a prop?—Do you know me, father?

OLD GOBBO.

Alack the day, I know you not, young gentleman: but, I pray you, tell me, is my boy—God rest his soul!—alive or dead?

LAUNCELOT GOBBO.

Do you not know me, father?

OLD GOBBO.

Alack, sir, I am sand-blind; I know you not.

---

[1] *ergo:* therefore.
[2] Sisters Three: the Fates—Clotho, Lachesis, and Atropos—who controlled human destiny.

LAUNCELOT GOBBO.

Nay, indeed, if you had your eyes, you might fail of the knowing me: it is a wise father that knows his own child.[1] Well, old man, I will tell you news of your son: give me your blessing [*kneels*]: truth will come to light; murder cannot be hid long,—a man's son may; but, in the end, truth will out.

OLD GOBBO.

Pray you, sir, stand up: I am sure you are not Launcelot, my boy.

LAUNCELOT GOBBO.

Pray you, let's have no more fooling about it, but give me your blessing: I am Launcelot, your boy that was, your son that is, your child that shall be.

OLD GOBBO.

I cannot think you are my son.

LAUNCELOT GOBBO.

I know not what I shall think of that: but I am Launcelot, the Jew's man; and I am sure Margery your wife is my mother.

OLD GOBBO.

Her name is Margery, indeed: I'll be sworn, if thou be Launcelot, thou art mine own flesh and blood. Lord worshipt might he be! what a beard hast thou got![2] thou hast got more hair on thy chin than Dobbin my fill-horse[3] has on his tail.

LAUNCELOT GOBBO [*rising*].

It should seem, then, that Dobbin's tail grows backward; I am sure he had more hair of his tail than I have of my face when I last saw him.

---

[1] it is a wise father that knows his own child: this is a twisted version of the proverb: " 'Tis a wise child that knows his own father."
[2] what a beard hast thou got: Launcelot has turned his head so that his father feels his long hair and thinks it is a beard.
[3] fill-horse: a cart horse that draws between shafts or thills (fills).

OLD GOBBO.

Lord, how art thou changed! How dost thou and thy master
agree? I have brought him a present. How 'gree you now?

LAUNCELOT GOBBO.

Well, well: but, for mine own part, as I have set up my rest[1]
to run away, so I will not rest till I have run some ground.[2]
My master's a very Jew:[3] give him a present! give him a
halter:[4] I am famisht in his service; you may tell[5] every
finger I have with my ribs. Father, I am glad you are come:
give me your present to one Master Bassanio, who, indeed,
gives rare new liveries: if I serve not him, I will run as far as
God has any ground.—O rare fortune! here comes the man:
—to him, father; for I am a Jew, if I serve the Jew any
longer.

Enter BASSANIO, *with* LEONARDO *and a* FOLLOWER *or two.*

BASSANIO.

You may do so;—but let it be so hasted,[6] that supper be
ready at the furthest by five of the clock. See these letters
deliver'd; put the liveries to making; and desire Gratiano to
come anon to my lodging.   [*Exit a* SERVANT.

LAUNCELOT GOBBO.

To him, father.

OLD GOBBO.

God bless your worship!

BASSANIO.

Gramercy:[7] wouldst thou aught with me?

---

[1] set up my rest: decided to risk everything (as in gambling).
[2] some ground: some distance. [3] a very Jew: a Jew in every respect.
[4] halter: noose. [5] tell: count. [6] hasted: timed. [7] Gramercy: a corruption of *grant merci*, a French phrase meaning great, or many,
thanks.

OLD GOBBO.

Here's my son, sir, a poor boy,—

LAUNCELOT GOBBO.

Not a poor boy, sir, but the rich Jew's man; that would, sir,
—as my father shall specify,—

OLD GOBBO.

He hath a great infection,[1] sir, as one would say, to serve,—

LAUNCELOT GOBBO.

Indeed, the short and the long is, I serve the Jew, and have a
desire,—as my father shall specify,—

OLD GOBBO.

His master and he—saving your worship's reverence—are
scarce cater-cousins,[2]—

LAUNCELOT GOBBO.

To be brief, the very truth is, that the Jew having done me
wrong, doth cause me,—as my father, being, I hope, an old
man, shall frutify[3] unto you,—

OLD GOBBO.

I have here a dish of doves that I would bestow upon your
worship; and my suit is,—

LAUNCELOT GOBBO.

In very brief, the suit is impertinent[4] to myself, as your worship shall know by this honest old man; and, though I say
it, though old man, yet poor man, my father.

BASSANIO.

One speak for both.—What would you?

LAUNCELOT GOBBO.

Serve you, sir.

OLD GOBBO.

That is the very defect[5] of the matter, sir.

---

[1] **infection:** desire or affection. [2] **scarce cater-cousins:** not closely
related; that is, they do not often agree. [3] **frutify:** Launcelot is
trying to use big words and doesn't know how; he probably
wanted to say fructify, although his meaning was signify. [4] **impertinent:** pertinent; appurtenant. [5] **defect:** effect (purport).

BASSANIO.

I know thee well; thou hast obtain'd thy suit:
Shylock thy master spoke with me this day,
And hath preferr'd thee,[1]—if it be preferment
To leave a rich Jew's service, to become
The follower of so poor a gentleman.

LAUNCELOT GOBBO.

The old proverb[2] is very well parted between my master
Shylock and you, sir: you have the grace of God, sir, and he
hath enough.

BASSANIO.

Thou speak'st it well.—Go, father, with thy son.—
Take leave of thy old master, and inquire
My lodging out.—Give him a livery
More guarded [3] than his fellows': see it done.

LAUNCELOT GOBBO.

Father, in.—I cannot get a service, no;—I have ne'er a tongue
in my head.—Well [*looking on his palm*], if any man in Italy
have a fairer table,[4] which doth offer to swear upon a book,
I shall have good fortune!—Go to, here's a simple line of life!
here's a small trifle of wives! alas, fifteen wives is nothing!
eleven widows and nine maids is a simple coming-in[5] for one
man; and then to scape[6] drowning thrice, and to be in peril
of my life with the edge of a feather-bed,[7]—here are simple
scapes! Well, if Fortune be a woman, she's a good wench for
this gear.—Father, come; I'll take my leave of the Jew in
the twinkling of an eye.   [*Exeunt* LAUNCELOT *and* OLD GOBBO.

---

[1] **preferr'd thee:** recommended you for advancement.   [2] **The old proverb:** "He that hath the grace of God, hath enough."   [3] **guarded:** trimmed with braid.   [4] **table:** palm; the lines in the hand used for telling one's fortune.   [5] **simple coming-in:** a mere trifle in income, in the form of dowries.   [6] **scape:** escape.   [7] **feather-bed:** marriage bed.

BASSANIO.

I pray thee, good Leonardo, think on this:
These things being bought and orderly bestow'd,
Return in haste, for I do feast to-night
My best-esteem'd acquaintance: hie thee, go.

LEONARDO.

My best endeavours shall be done herein.

Enter GRATIANO.

GRATIANO.

Where's your master?

LEONARDO.

           Yonder, sir, he walks.   [*Exit.*

GRATIANO.

Signior Bassanio,—

BASSANIO.

Gratiano!

GRATIANO.

I have a suit to you.[1]

BASSANIO.

          You have obtain'd it.

GRATIANO.

You must not deny me: I must go with you to Belmont.

BASSANIO.

Why, then you must. But hear thee, Gratiano:
Thou art too wild, too rude, and bold of voice,—
Parts[2] that become thee happily enough,
And in such eyes as ours appear not faults;
But where thou art not known, why, there they show
Something too liberal.[3] Prithee, take pain
To allay with some cold drops of modesty[4]

---

[1] a suit to you: a favor to ask of you.
[2] Parts: traits of character.
[3] liberal: unrestrained.
[4] modesty: moderation.

Thy skipping spirit;[1] lest, through thy wild behaviour,
I be misconstred [2] in the place I go to,
And lose my hopes.

GRATIANO.

Signior Bassanio, hear me:
If I do not put on a sober habit,[3]
Talk with respect, and swear but now and then,
Wear prayer-books in my pocket, look demurely;
Nay, more, while grace is saying, hood mine eyes
Thus with my hat, and sigh, and say amen;
Use all the observance of civility,
Like one well studied in a sad ostent[4]
To please his grandam,—never trust me more.

BASSANIO.

Well, we shall see your bearing.

GRATIANO.

Nay, but I bar to-night: you shall not gauge me
By what we do to-night.

BASSANIO.

No, that were pity:
I would entreat you rather to put on
Your boldest suit of mirth, for we have friends
That purpose merriment.[5] But fare ye well:
I have some business.

GRATIANO.

And I must to Lorenzo and the rest:
But we will visit you at supper-time.   [*Exeunt.*

---

[1] **skipping spirit:** boisterous spirits.
[2] **misconstred:** misconstrued; misjudged.
[3] **put on a sober habit:** assume an air of gravity.
[4] **sad ostent:** sober display or appearance.
[5] **purpose merriment:** propose to have a good time.

SCENE III.

A room in SHYLOCK's *house.*

Enter JESSICA AND LAUNCELOT.

JESSICA.

I am sorry thou wilt leave my father so:
Our house is hell: and thou, a merry devil,
Didst rob it of some taste of tediousness.
But fare thee well; there is a ducat for thee:
And, Launcelot, soon at supper shalt thou see
Lorenzo, who is thy new master's guest:
Give him this letter; do it secretly;—
And so farewell: I would not have my father
See me in talk with thee.

LAUNCELOT GOBBO.

Adieu; tears exhibit my tongue.[1] Most beautiful pagan, most
sweet Jew! if a Christian did not play the knave and get thee,
I am much deceived. But, adieu: these foolish drops[2] do
something drown my manly spirit: adieu.

JESSICA.

Farewell, good Launcelot.—   [*Exit* LAUNCELOT.
Alack, what heinous sin is it in me
To be ashamed to be my father's child!
But though I am a daughter to his blood,
I am not to his manners.[3] O Lorenzo,
If thou keep promise, I shall end this strife,—
Become a Christian, and thy loving wife!   [*Exit.*

---

[1] **exhibit my tongue:** restrain; Launcelot mistakes the word "exhibit" for "inhibit."
[2] **foolish drops:** his way of apologizing for his tears.
[3] **manners:** character.

Scene IV.

Venice. A street.

Enter GRATIANO, LORENZO, SALARINO, *and* SOLANIO.

LORENZO.
Nay, we will slink away in supper-time,
Disguise us at my lodging, and return
All in an hour.

GRATIANO.
We have not made good preparation.

SALARINO.
We have not spoke us yet of torch-bearers.

SOLANIO.
'Tis vile, unless it may be quaintly order'd,[1]
And better in my mind not undertook.

LORENZO.
'Tis now but four o'clock: we have two hours
To furnish us.[2]

Enter LAUNCELOT, *with a letter.*

Friend Launcelot, what's the news?

LAUNCELOT GOBBO.
An it shall please you to break up[3] this, it shall seem to signify.

LORENZO.
I know the hand: in faith, 'tis a fair hand;
And whiter than the paper it writ on
Is the fair hand that writ.

GRATIANO.
                          Love-news, in faith.

LAUNCELOT GOBBO.
By your leave, sir.

---

[1] quaintly order'd: well-planned; carried out with attention to the smallest detail.
[2] to furnish us: to get ready.
[3] break up: open.

LORENZO.

Whither goest thou?

LAUNCELOT GOBBO.

Marry, sir, to bid my old master the Jew to sup to-night with
my new master the Christian.

LORENZO.

Hold here, take this [*gives money*]:—tell gentle Jessica
I will not fail her; speak it privately; go.— [*Exit* LAUNCELOT.
Gentlemen, will you prepare you for this mask[1] to-night?
I am provided of a torch-bearer.

SALARINO.

Ay, marry, I'll be gone about it straight.[2]

SOLANIO.

And so will I.

LORENZO.

Meet me and Gratiano
At Gratiano's lodging some hour hence.[3]

SALARINO.

'Tis good we do so.   [*Exeunt* SALARINO *and* SOLANIO.

GRATIANO.

Was not that letter from fair Jessica?

LORENZO.

I must needs tell thee all. She hath directed
How I shall take her from her father's house;
What gold and jewels she is furnisht with;
What page's suit she hath in readiness:
If e'er the Jew her father come to heaven,
It will be for his gentle daughter's sake:

---

[1] **mask:** masquerade ball in which dancing, music, and pantomime
play a part.
[2] **straight:** immediately.
[3] **some hour hence:** about an hour from now.

And never dare misfortune cross her foot,[1]
Unless she do it under this excuse,—
That she is issue to a faithless Jew.
Come, go with me: peruse this as thou goest:
Fair Jessica shall be my torch-bearer.   [*Exeunt.*

Scene V.

The same. Before shylock's *house.*

Enter shylock *and* launcelot.

shylock.

Well, thou shalt see,.thy eyes shall be thy judge,
The difference of old Shylock and Bassanio:—
What, Jessica!—thou shalt not gormandize,[2]
As thou hast done with me;—what, Jessica!—
And sleep and snore, and rend apparel out;—
Why, Jessica, I say!

launcelot gobbo.
                    Why, Jessica!

shylock.
Who bids thee call? I do not bid thee call.

launcelot gobbo.
Your worship was wont to tell me that I could do nothing
without bidding.

Enter jessica.

jessica.
Call you? what is your will?

shylock.
I am bid forth to supper, Jessica:
There are my keys.—But wherefore should I go?
I am not bid for love; they flatter me:
But yet I'll go in hate, to feed upon

---

[1] cross her foot: cross her path.
[2] gormandize: overeat.

The prodigal Christian.—Jessica, my girl,
Look to my house.—I am right loth to go:
There is some ill a-brewing towards my rest,
For I did dream of money-bags to-night.

    LAUNCELOT GOBBO.

I beseech you, sir, go: my young master doth expect your
reproach.[1]

    SHYLOCK.

So do I his.

    LAUNCELOT GOBBO.

And they have conspired together,—I will not say you shall
see a mask; but if you do, then it was not for nothing that
my nose fell a-bleeding on Black-Monday[2] last at six o'clock
i' th' morning, falling out that year on Ash-Wednesday was
four year,[3] in th' afternoon.

    SHYLOCK.

What, are there masks?—Hear you me, Jessica:
Lock up my doors; and when you hear the drum,
And the vile squealing of the wry-neckt fife,
Clamber not you up to the casements then,
Nor thrust your head into the public street,
To gaze on Christian fools with varnish faces;[4]
But stop my house's ears, I mean my casements:
Let not the sound of shallow foppery[5] enter
My sober house.—By Jacob's staff, I swear
I have no mind of feasting forth to-night:
But I will go.—Go you before me, sirrah;
Say I will come.

    LAUNCELOT GOBBO.

          I will go before, sir.—
Mistress, look out at window for all this;[6]

---

[1] reproach: approach. [2] Black-Monday: Easter Monday. [3] Ash-Wednesday was/four year: it was four years ago last Ash Wednesday. [4] varnisht faces: faces covered with varnished masks. [5] foppery: foolishness. [6] for all this: in spite of this.

There will come a Christian by
Will be worth a Jewess' eye.   [*Exit.*

SHYLOCK.

What says that fool of Hagar's offspring,[1] ha?

JESSICA.

His words were, 'Farewell, mistress;' nothing else.

SHYLOCK.

The patch[2] is kind enough; but a huge feeder,
Snail-slow in profit,[3] and he sleeps by day
More than the wild-cat: drones hive not with me;
Therefore I part with him; and part with him
To one that I would have him help to waste
His borrow'd purse.—Well, Jessica, go in:
Perhaps I will return immediately:
Do as I bid you; shut doors after you:
Fast bind, fast find,—
A proverb never stale in thrifty mind.   [*Exit.*

JESSICA.

Farewell; and if my fortune be not crost,
I have a father, you a daughter, lost.   [*Exit.*

Enter the Maskers GRATIANO *and* SALARINO.

GRATIANO.

This is the pent-house[4] under which Lorenzo
Desired us to make stand.[5]

SALARINO.

His hour is almost past.

GRATIANO.

And it is marvel he out-dwells his hour,[6]
For lovers ever run before the clock.[7]

SALARINO.

O, ten times faster Venus' pigeons fly

---

[1] **Hagar's offspring:** one of the outcasts (Hagar and her son Ishmael were driven into the desert because of the jealousy of her mistress, Sarah, wife of Abraham). [2] **patch:** fool. [3] **in profit:** in doing anything profitable. [4] **pent-house:** lean-to. [5] **make stand:** wait. [6] **out-dwells his hour:** he is late in coming. [7] **run before the clock:** arrives early, before the appointed time.

To seal love's bonds new-made than they are wont
To keep obliged faith unforfeited!

GRATIANO.

That ever holds: who riseth from a feast
With that keen appetite that he sits down?
Where is the horse that doth untread again
His tedious measures[1] with the unbated fire
That he did pace them first? All things that are,
Are with more spirit chased than enjoy'd.
How like a younker[2] or a prodigal
The scarfed bark[3] puts from her native bay,
Hugg'd and embraced by the strumpet wind!
How like a prodigal doth she return,
With over-weather'd ribs, and ragged sails,
Lean, rent, and beggar'd by the strumpet wind!

SALARINO.

Here comes Lorenzo:—more of this hereafter.

Enter LORENZO.

LORENZO.

Sweet friends, your patience for my long abode;[4]
Not I, but my affairs, have made you wait:
When you shall please to play the thieves for wives,
I'll watch as long for you then.—Approach;
Here dwells my father Jew.—Ho! who's within?

Enter JESSICA, *above, in boy's clothes.*

JESSICA.

Who are you? Tell me, for more certainty,
Albeit I'll swear that I do know your tongue.

LORENZO.

Lorenzo, and thy love.

---

[1] tedious measures: dancing steps that horses were trained to perform.
[2] younker: young gentleman; in this case, probably younger son.
[3] scarfed bark: ship decked with flags and pennants.
[4] long abode: long delay.

JESSICA.

Lorenzo, certain; and my love, indeed,—
For who love I so much? And now who knows
But you, Lorenzo, whether I am yours?

LORENZO.

Heaven and thy thoughts are witness that thou art.

JESSICA.

Here, catch this casket; it is worth the pains.
I am glad 'tis night, you do not look on me,
For I am much ashamed of my exchange:[1]
But love is blind, and lovers cannot see
The pretty follies that themselves commit;
For if they could, Cupid himself would blush
To see me thus transformed to a boy.

LORENZO.

Descend, for you must be my torch-bearer.

JESSICA.

What, must I hold a candle to my shames?
They in themselves, good sooth, are too-too light[2]
Why, 'tis an office of discovery,[3] love;
And I should be obscured.[4]

LORENZO.

                  So are you, sweet,
Even in the lovely garnish[5] of a boy.
But come at once;
For the close[6] night doth play the runaway,
And we are stay'd for[7] at Bassanio's feast.

JESSICA.

I will make fast the doors, and gild myself
With some moe[8] ducats, and be with you straight.

                             [*Exit above.*

---

[1] **exchange:** change of clothes. [2] **too-too light:** too frivolous; too glaring. [3] **office of discovery:** acting as a torchbearer might cause her to be discovered. [4] **obscured:** hidden. [5] **garnish:** attire. [6] **close:** favorable to concealment. [7] **stayed for:** awaited. [8] **moe:** more.

GRATIANO.

Now, by my hood,[1] a Gentile, and no Jew.

LORENZO.

Beshrew me[2] but I love her heartily;
For she is wise, if I can judge of her;
And fair she is, if that mine eyes be true;
And true she is, as she hath proved herself;
And therefore, like herself, wise, fair, and true,
Shall she be placed in my constant soul.

Enter JESSICA, *below.*

What, art thou come?—On, gentlemen; away!
Our masking mates by this time for us stay.

                [*Exit with* JESSICA *and* SALARINO.

Enter ANTONIO.

ANTONIO.

Who's there?

GRATIANO.

Signior Antonio!

ANTONIO.

Fie, fie, Gratiano! where are all the rest?
'Tis nine o'clock; our friends all stay for you.
No mask to-night: the wind is come about;[3]
Bassanio presently will go aboard:
I have sent twenty out to seek for you.

GRATIANO.

I am glad on't: I desire no more delight
Than to be under sail and gone to-night.   [*Exeunt.*

---

[1] by my hood: a mild oath.
[2] Beshrew me: curse me.
[3] is come about: has changed.

Scene VI.

Belmont. A room in PORTIA's *house.*

Enter PORTIA, *with the* PRINCE OF MOROCCO, *and their* TRAINS. *Flourish cornets.*

PORTIA.
Go draw aside the curtains, and discover[1]
The several caskets to this noble prince.—
Now make your choice.
PRINCE OF MOROCCO.
The first, of gold, which this inscription bears,—
'Who chooseth me shall gain what many men desire;'
The second, silver, which this promise carries,—
'Who chooseth me shall get as much as he deserves;'
This third, dull lead, with warning all as blunt,—
'Who chooseth me must give and hazard all he hath.'—
How shall I know if I do choose the right?
PORTIA.
The one of them contains my picture, prince:
If you choose that, then I am yours withal.[2]
PRINCE OF MOROCCO.
Some god direct my judgement! Let me see;
I will survey the inscriptions back again.[3]
What says this leaden casket?
'Who chooseth me must give and hazard all he hath.'
Must give,—for what? for lead? hazard for lead?
This casket threatens: men that hazard all
Do it in hope of fair advantages:
A golden mind stoops not to shows of dross;[4]

---

[1] discover: reveal.
[2] withal: at the same time.
[3] back again: from the last to the first.
[4] shows of dross: worthless-seeming objects.

I'll then nor give nor hazard aught for lead.
What says the silver, with her virgin hue? [1]
'Who chooseth me shall get as much as he deserves.'
As much as he deserves!—Pause there, Morocco,
And weigh thy value with an even hand:
If thou be'st rated by thy estimation,[2]
Thou dost deserve enough; and yet enough
May not extend so far as to the lady:
And yet to be afeard of my deserving,
Were but a weak disabling[3] of myself.
As much as I deserve!—Why, that's the lady:
I do in birth deserve her, and in fortunes,
In graces, and in qualities of breeding;
But more than these, in love I do deserve.
What if I stray'd no further, but chose here?—
Let's see once more this saying graved [4] in gold:
'Who chooseth me shall gain what many men desire.'
Why, that's the lady! all the world desires her;
From the four corners of the earth they come,
To kiss this shrine, this mortal-breathing saint:
The Hyrcanian deserts and the vasty wilds
Of wide Arabia are as throughfares now
For princes to come view fair Portia:
The watery kingdom,[5] whose ambitious head
Spits in the face of heaven, is no bar
To stop the foreign spirits;[6] but they come,
As o'er a brook, to see fair Portia.
One of these three contains her heavenly picture.
Is't like that lead contains her? 'Twere damnation
To think so base a thought: it were too gross[7]

---

[1] **virgin hue:** silver is the color of the moon, over which Diana, the virgin goddess, rules. [2] **rated by thy estimate:** valued according to your reputation. [3] **weak disabling:** undervaluation. [4] **graved:** engraved. [5] **watery kingdom:** the ocean. [6] **spirits:** spirited persons. [7] **gross:** coarse.

To rib her cerecloth[1] in the obscure[2] grave.
Or shall I think in silver she's immured,
Being ten times undervalued to tried gold?
O sinful thought! Never so rich a gem
Was set in worse than gold. They have in England
A coin that bears the figure of an angel [3]
Stamped in gold,—but that's insculpt[4] upon;
But here an angel [5] in a golden bed
Lies all within.—Deliver me the key:
Here do I choose, and thrive I as I may!

> PORTIA.

There, take it, prince; and if my form lie there,
Then I am yours.   [*He opens the golden casket.*

> PRINCE OF MOROCCO.

                    O hell! what have we here?
A carrion Death, within whose empty eye
There is a written scroll! I'll read the writing.

> All that glisters[6] is not gold,—
> Often have you heard that told:
> Many a man his life hath sold
> But my outside to behold:
> Gilded tombs do worms infold.
> Had you been as wise as bold,
> Young in limbs, in judgement old,
> Your answer had not been inscroll'd:[7]
> Fare you well; your suit is cold.

Cold, indeed; and labour lost:
    Then, farewell, heat; and welcome, frost! [8]—
Portia, adieu. I have too grieved a heart
To take a tedious leave: thus losers part.[9]

                    [*Exit with his* TRAIN. *Cornets.*

---

[1] cerecloth: cloth in which a corpse is wrapped. [2] obscure: hidden.
[3] angel: coin known by this name. [4] insculpt: engraved. [5] an angel:
Portia's portrait. [6] glisters: glistens. [7] inscroll'd: written on this
scroll. [8] farewell heat; and welcome, frost: since he has vowed
never to marry, love is now denied him. [9] part: depart.

PORTIA.

A gentle riddance.—Draw the curtains, go.—
Let all of his complexion[1] choose me so.   [*Exeunt.*

Scene VII.

Venice. A street.

Enter SALARINO *and* SOLANIO.

SALARINO.

Why, man, I saw Bassanio under sail:
With him is Gratiano gone along;
And in their ship I am sure Lorenzo is not.

SOLANIO.

The villain Jew with outcries raised the duke;
Who went with him to search Bassanio's ship.

SALARINO.

He came too late, the ship was under sail:
But there the duke was given to understand
That in a gondola were seen together
Lorenzo and his amorous Jessica:
Besides, Antonio certified the duke
They were not with Bassanio in his ship.

SOLANIO.

I never heard a passion so confused,
So strange, outrageous, and so variable,
As the dog Jew did utter in the streets:
'My daughter!—O my ducats!—O my daughter!
Fled with a Christian!—O my Christian ducats!—
Justice! the law! my ducats, and my daughter!
A sealed bag, two sealed bags of ducats,
Of double ducats,[2] stol'n from me by my daughter!
And jewels,—two stones, two rich and precious stones,
Stol'n by my daughter!—Justice! find the girl!

---

[1] **his complexion:** his like, or ilk.
[2] **double ducats:** ducats worth twice the value of the usual ones.

She hath the stones upon her, and the ducats!'

SALARINO.

Why, all the boys in Venice follow him,
Crying,—his stones, his daughter, and his ducats.

SOLANIO.

Let good Antonio look he keep his day,[1]
Or he shall pay for this.

SALARINO.

                    Marry, well remember'd,
I reason'd [2] with a Frenchman yesterday,
Who told me,—in the narrow seas that part
The French and English, there miscarried [3]
A vessel of our country richly fraught:[4]
I thought upon Antonio when he told me;
And wisht in silence that it were not his.

SOLANIO.

You were best to tell Antonio what you hear;
Yet do not suddenly, for it may grieve him.

SALARINO.

A kinder gentleman treads not the earth.
I saw Bassanio and Antonio part:
Bassanio told him he would make some speed
Of his return: he answer'd, 'Do not so,—
Slubber[5] not business for my sake, Bassanio,
But stay the very riping of the time;
And for the Jew's bond which he hath of me,
Let it not enter in your mind of love:[6]
Be merry; and employ your chiefest thoughts
To courtship, and such fair ostents[7] of love
As shall conveniently become you there:'
And even there, his eye being big with tears,
Turning his face, he put his hand behind him,

---

[1] **keep his day**: repays the money he owes Shylock promptly when due. [2] **reason'd**: talked. [3] **miscarried**: was lost. [4] **fraught**: freighted or laden. [5] **Slubber**: perform carelessly; bungle. [6] **your mind of love**: your loving mind. [7] **ostents**: displays; shows.

And with affection wondrous sensible[1]
He wrung Bassanio's hand; and so they parted.

SOLANIO.

I think he only loves the world for him.
I pray thee, let us go and find him out,
And quicken his embraced heaviness[2]
With some delight or other.

SALARINO.

                    Do we so.   [*Exeunt.*

SCENE VIII.

Belmont. A room in PORTIA'S *house.*

Enter NERISSA *and a* SERVITOR.

NERISSA.

Quick, quick, I pray thee; draw the curtain straight:
The Prince of Arragon hath ta'en his oath,
And comes to his election[3] presently.

Enter PRINCE OF ARRAGON, *his* TRAIN, *and*
PORTIA. *Flourish cornets.*

PORTIA.

Behold, there stand the caskets, noble prince:
If you choose that wherein I am contain'd,
Straight shall our nuptial rites be solemnized:
But if you fail, without more speech, my lord,
You must be gone from hence immediately.

PRINCE OF ARRAGON.

I am enjoin'd by oath to observe three things:—
First, never to unfold to any one
Which casket 'twas I chose; next, if I fail
Of the right casket, never in my life

---

[1] **with affection wondrous sensible**: visibly moved by great emotion.
[2] **quicken his embraced heaviness**: cheer him out of his self-imposed sadness.
[3] **election**: choice.

To woo a maid in way of marriage; lastly,
If I do fail in fortune of my choice,
Immediately to leave you and be gone.

    PORTIA.

To these injunctions every one doth swear
That comes to hazard for my worthless self.

    PRINCE OF ARRAGON.

And so have I addrest me.[1] Fortune now
To my heart's hope!—Gold, silver, and base lead.
'Who chooseth me must give and hazard all he hath.'
You shall look fairer, ere I give or hazard.
What says the golden chest? ha! let me see:
'Who chooseth me shall gain what many men desire.'
What many men desire!—that many may be meant
By the fool multitude, that choose by show,
Not learning more than the fond [2] eye doth teach;
Which pries not to th' interior,[3] but, like the martlet,[4]
Builds in the weather on the outward wall,
Even in the force and road of casualty.[5]
I will not choose what many men desire,
Because I will not jump with common spirits,
And rank me with the barbarous multitudes.
Why, then to thee, thou silver treasure-house;
Tell me once more what title thou dost bear:
'Who chooseth me shall get as much as he deserves:'
And well said too; for who shall go about
To cozen[6] fortune, and be honourable

---

[1] addrest me: applied myself to this matter. [2] fond: foolish. [3] pries not to th' interior: does not go to the heart of the matter. [4] martlet: the European martin (the "temple-haunting" bird of Macbeth). [5] in the force and road of casualty: exposed to every hazard; in the very pathway of destructive forces. [6] cozen: cheat.

Without the stamp of merit? Let none presume
To wear an undeserved dignity.
O, that estates, degrees, and offices,
Were not derived corruptly! and that clear[1] honour
Were purchased by the merit of the wearer!
How many then should cover[2] that stand bare!
How many be commanded that command!
How much low peasantry would then be glean'd
From the true seed of honour! [3] and how much honour
Pickt from the chaff and ruin of the times,
To be new-varnisht! Well, but to my choice:
'Who chooseth me shall get as much as he deserves.'
I will assume desert.—Give me a key for this,
And instantly unlock my fortunes here.

[*He opens the silver casket*

PORTIA [*aside*].
Too long a pause for that which you find here.
PRINCE OF ARRAGON.
What's here? the portrait of a blinking idiot,
Presenting me a schedule! [4] I will read it.
How much unlike art thou to Portia!
How much unlike my hopes and my deservings!
'Who chooseth me shall have as much as he deserves.'
Did I deserve no more than a fool's head?
Is that my prize? are my deserts no better?
PORTIA.
To offend, and judge, are distinct offices,
And of opposed natures.
PRINCE OF ARRAGON.
                              What is here?

---

[1] clear: unspotted.
[2] should cover: would put on their hats.
[3] true seed of honour: the nobility.
[4] schedule: scroll.

The fire seven times tried [1] this:
Seven times tried that judgement is,
That did never choose amiss.
Some there be that shadows kiss;
Such have but a shadow's bliss.
There be fools alive, I wis,[2]
Silver'd o'er;[3] and so was this.
Take what wife you will to bed,
I will ever be your head:[4]
So be gone; you are sped.[5]

Still more fool I shall appear
By the time I linger here:[6]
With one fool's head I came to woo,
But I go away with two.—
Sweet, adieu. I'll keep my oath,
Patiently to bear my wroth.[7]   [*Exit with his* TRAIN.

PORTIA.
Thus hath the candle singed the moth.
O, these deliberate fools! when they do choose,
They have the wisdom by their wit to lose.

NERISSA.
The ancient saying is no heresy,—
Hanging and wiving goes by destiny.

PORTIA.
Come, draw the curtain, Nerissa.

Enter a SERVANT.

SERVANT.
Where is my lady?
PORTIA.
                Here: what would my lord?

---

[1] tried: tempered; refined. [2] I wis: I know. [3] Silver'd o'er: silver plated; misleading appearance of worth. [4] I will ever be your head: you will always be a fool. [5] sped: finished. [6] By the time I linger here: the longer I stay here. [7] wroth: chagrin.

SERVANT.

Madam, there is alighted at your gate
A young Venetian, one that comes before
To signify th' approaching of his lord;
From whom he bringeth sensible regreets,[1]
To wit, besides commends[2] and courteous breath[3]
Gifts of rich value. Yet I have not seen
So likely[4] an ambassador of love:
A day in April never came so sweet,
To show how costly[5] summer was at hand,
As this fore-spurrer[6] comes before his lord.

PORTIA.

No more, I pray thee: I am half afeard
Thou wilt say anon he is some kin to thee,
Thou spend'st such high-day wit[7] in praising him.—
Come, come, Nerissa; for I long to see
Quick Cupid's post[8] that comes so mannerly.

NERISSA.

Bassanio, lord Love, if thy will it be!   [*Exeunt.*

---

[1] **sensible regreets**: sincere greetings. [2] **commends**: regards. [3] **breath**: speech. [4] **likely**: promising. [5] **costly**: bountiful [6] **fore-spurrer**: advance rider. [7] **high-day wit**: wit befitting a feast day [8] **post**: messenger.

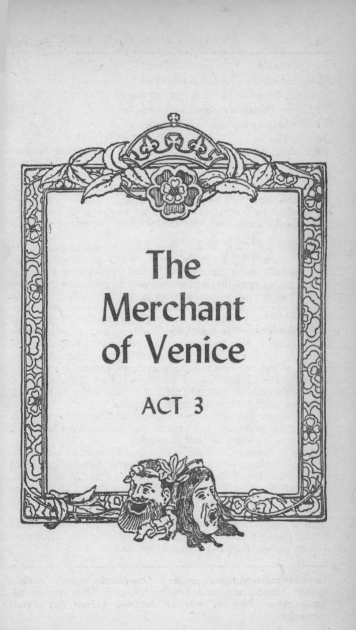

The Merchant of Venice

ACT 3

ACT III

In Venice, Solanio and Salarino discuss rumors that Antonio has lost a ship. Shylock enters and accuses them of helping his daughter to escape. He strongly reaffirms his intention to have a pound of Antonio's flesh if the merchant forfeits. Since the Christians teach him revenge, he argues, he will practice it. As the two Venetians leave to go to Antonio, Tubal, another Jew, enters, and Shylock tells him bitterly of Jessica's thefts.

At Belmont, Portia tries to persuade Bassanio to put off the fateful choice. Bassanio, however, wants to choose immediately. Expressing disdain for the deceptiveness of gold and silver, he chooses the lead casket and is rewarded with the portrait of Portia, who gives him a ring which he swears to keep until his death. In the meantime, Gratiano has been wooing Nerissa and now asks Bassanio's permission to marry at the same time. Lorenzo and Jessica enter, together with Salarino, who gives Bassanio a most disturbing letter from Antonio. All of Antonio's ships have suffered disaster; he has no money to pay the bond, and Shylock now demands his pound of flesh. Portia, learning of the debt, offers gold to pay it twenty times over. Bassanio reads Antonio's letter to her and, with her good wishes, leaves for Venice.

In Venice, Shylock meets Salarino and Antonio with his jailer in the street. Shylock repeats that he will have his bond, and Antonio resigns himself to death.

Back in Belmont, Portia gives the management of her household to Lorenzo, telling him that she and Nerissa will be in a monastery two miles away. She sends a letter to her cousin, Doctor Bellario, in Padua, and tells Nerissa that they will disguise themselves as young men and go to Venice after their husbands.

In a comic scene, Launcelot, Jessica, and Lorenzo joke about Jessica's conversion and about the serving of dinner. Jessica praises Portia as a matchless woman.

ACT III. Scene I.

Venice A street

Enter SOLANIO *and* SALARINO.

SOLANIO.
Now, what news on the Rialto?

SOLANIO.
Why, yet it lives there uncheckt,[1] that Antonio hath a ship of rich lading wrackt[2] on the narrow seas; the Goodwins,[3] I think they call the place; a very dangerous flat and fatal, where the carcasses of many a tall ship lie buried, as they say, if my gossip Report be an honest woman of her word.

SOLANIO.
I would she were as lying a gossip in that as ever knapt ginger,[4] or made her neighbours believe she wept for the death of a third husband. But it is true,—without any slips of prolixity,[5] or crossing the plain highway of talk,—that the good Antonio, the honest Antonio,——O, that I had a title good enough to keep his name company!—

SALARINO.
Come, the full stop.

SOLANIO.
Ha,—what sayest thou?—Why, the end is, he hath lost a ship.

SALARINO.
I would it might prove the end of his losses.

SOLANIO.
Let me say amen betimes, lest the devil cross my prayer,— for here he comes in the likeness of a Jew.

Enter SHYLOCK.

How now, Shylock! what news among the merchants?

---

[1] **yet it lives there uncheckt:** yet the rumor circulates there without being denied or challenged. [2] **wrackt:** wrecked. [3] **the Goodwins:** the Goodwin Sands, a dangerous shoal in the English Channel (the narrow seas). [4] **knapt ginger:** nibbled on ginger root. [5] **without any slips/of prolixity:** without any slips of the tongue due to longwindedness.

SHYLOCK.

You knew, none so well, none so well as you, of my daughter's flight.

SALARINO.

That's certain: I, for my part, knew the tailor that made the wings she flew withal.

SOLANIO.

And Shylock, for his own part, knew the bird was fledged;[1] and then it is the complexion[2] of them all to leave the dam.[3]

SHYLOCK.

She is damn'd for it.

SALARINO.

That's certain, if the devil may be her judge.

SHYLOCK.

My own flesh and blood to rebel!

SOLANIO.

Out upon it, old carrion! rebels it[4] at these years?

SHYLOCK.

I say my daughter is my flesh and blood.

SALARINO.

There is more difference between thy flesh and hers than between jet and ivory; more between your bloods than there is between red wine and rhenish.[5]—But tell us, do you hear whether Antonio have had any loss at sea or no?

SHYLOCK.

There I have another bad match: a bankrout,[6] a prodigal, who dare scarce show his head on the Rialto;—a beggar, that was used to come so smug upon the mart;—let him look to his bond; he was wont to call me usurer;—let him look to his

---

[1] fledged: ready to take wing.
[2] complexion: nature; disposition.
[3] dam: parent.
[4] rebels it: Solanio pretends to misunderstand Shylock.
[5] rhenish: white wine.
[6] bankrout: bankrupt.

bond: he was wont to lend money for a Christian courtesy:—
let him look to his bond.

SALARINO.

Why, I am sure, if he forfeit, thou wilt not take his flesh:
what's that good for?

SHYLOCK.

To bait fish withal: if it will feed nothing else, it will feed my
revenge. He hath disgraced me, and hinder'd me half a million;[1] laught at my losses, mockt at my gains, scorn'd my
nation, thwarted my bargains, cooled my friends, heated mine
enemies: and what's his reason? I am a Jew. Hath not a Jew
eyes? hath not a Jew hands, organs, dimensions, senses, affections, passions? fed with the same food, hurt with the same
weapons, subject to the same diseases, heal'd by the same
means, warm'd and cool'd by the same winter and summer,
as a Christian is? If you prick us, do we not bleed? if you
tickle us, do we not laugh? if you poison us, do we not die?
and if you wrong us, shall we not revenge? if we are like you
in the rest, we will resemble you in that. If a Jew wrong a
Christian, what is his humility?[2] revenge: if a Christian
wrong a Jew, what should his sufferance be by Christian
example? why, revenge. The villainy you teach me, I will
execute; and it shall go hard but I will better the instruction.[3]

Enter a SERVANT *from* ANTONIO.

SERVANT.

Gentlemen, my master Antonio is at his house, and desires to
speak with you both.

SALARINO.

We have been up and down to seek him.

---

[1] **hinder'd me half a mil/lion:** prevented me from making a half-
million profit. [2] **what is his humility:** how much Christian benevo-
lence or love of humanity does he show. [3] **it shall go hard but I
will better the instruction:** it will be my fault if I do not improve
on the lessons that the Christians have taught me.

SOLANIO.

Here comes another of the tribe: a third cannot be matcht, unless the devil himself turn Jew.

[*Exeunt* SOLANIO, SALARINO, *and* SERVANT.

Enter TUBAL.

SHYLOCK.

How now, Tubal! what news from Genoa? hast thou found my daughter?

TUBAL.

I often came where I did hear of her, but cannot find her.

SHYLOCK.

Why, there, there, there, there! a diamond gone, cost me two thousand ducats in Frankfort! The curse never fell upon our nation till now; I never felt it till now:—two thousand ducats in that; and other precious, precious jewels.—I would my daughter were dead at my foot, and the jewels in her ear! would she were hearsed at my foot, and the ducats in her coffin! No news of them?—Why, so:—and I know not what's spent in the search: why, thou, loss upon loss! the thief gone with so much, and so much to find the thief; and no satisfaction, no revenge: nor no ill luck stirring but what lights on my shoulders; no sighs but of my breathing; no tears but of my shedding.

TUBAL.

Yes, other men have ill luck too: Antonio, as I heard in Genoa,—

SHYLOCK.

What, what, what? ill luck, ill luck?

TUBAL.

Hath an argosy cast away, coming from Tripolis.

SHYLOCK.

I thank God, I thank God!—Is't true, is't true?

TUBAL.

I spoke with some of the sailors that escaped the wrack.

SHYLOCK.

I thank thee, good Tubal:—good news, good news! ha, ha!—
where? in Genoa?

TUBAL.

Your daughter spent in Genoa, as I heard, one night fourscore
ducats.

SHYLOCK.

Thou stick'st a dagger in me:—I shall never see my gold
again: fourscore ducats at a sitting! fourscore ducats!

TUBAL.

There came divers[1] of Antonio's creditors in my company to
Venice, that swear he cannot choose but break.[2]

SHYLOCK.

I am very glad of it:—I'll plague him; I'll torture him:—I am
glad on't.[3]

TUBAL.

One of them show'd me a ring that he had of your daughter
for a monkey.

SHYLOCK.

Out upon her! Thou torturest me, Tubal: it was my turquoise;
I hald it of Leah[4] when I was a bachelor: I would not have
given it for a wilderness of monkeys.

TUBAL.

But Antonio is certainly undone.[5]

---

[1] divers: various.
[2] he cannot choose but break: he cannot avoid going bankrupt.
[3] on't: of it.
[4] Leah: Shylock's wife.
[5] undone: ruined; done for.

SHYLOCK.

Nay, that's true, that's very true. Go, Tubal, fee[1] me an of-
ficer; bespeak[2] him a fortnight before. I will have the heart of
him, if he forfeit; for, were he out of Venice, I can make what
merchandise I will.[3] Go, Tubal, and meet me at our synagogue; go, good Tubal; at our synagogue, Tubal.   [*Exeunt.*

SCENE II.

Belmont. A room in PORTIA'S *house.*

Enter BASSANIO, PORTIA, GRATIANO,
NERISSA, *and all their* TRAIN.

PORTIA.

I pray you, tarry: pause a day or two
Before you hazard; for, in choosing wrong,
I lose your company: therefore, forbear awhile.
There's something tells me—but it is not love—
I would not lose you; and you know yourself,
Hate counsels not in such a quality.[4]
But lest you should not understand me well,—
And yet a maiden hath no tongue[5] but thought,—
I would detain you here some month or two
Before you venture for me. I could teach you
How to choose right, but then I am forsworn;
So will I never be: so may you miss me;
But if you do, you'll make me wish a sin,
That I had been forsworn. Beshrew your eyes,
They have o'erlookt me,[6] and divided me?
One half of me is yours, the other half yours,—
Mine own, I would say; but if mine, then yours,
And so all yours! O, these naughty[7] times
Put bars between the owners and their rights!
And so, though yours, not yours.—Prove it so,

---

[1] **fee**: retain. [2] **bespeak**: hire. [3] **I can make what/merchandise I
will**: I can drive as hard a bargain as I wish. [4] **in such a quality**: in
such a way. [5] **a maiden hath no tongue**: it is not seemly for a
maiden to do much talking. [6] **o'erlookt me**: bewitched me.
[7] **naughty**: wicked.

Let fortune go to hell for it,—not I.
I speak too long; but 'tis to peize[1] the time,
To eke it, and to draw it out in length,
To stay you from election.[2]

　　BASSANIO.

　　　　　　　　　　Let me choose;
For, as I am, I live upon the rack.[3]

　　PORTIA.

Upon the rack, Bassanio! then confess
What treason[4] there is mingled with your love.

　　BASSANIO.

None but that ugly treason of mistrust,
Which makes me fear the enjoying of my love:
There may as well be amity and league
'Tween snow and fire, as treason and my love.

　　PORTIA.

Ay, but I fear you speak upon the rack,
Where men enforced [5] do speak any thing.

　　BASSANIO.

Promise me life, and I'll confess the truth.

　　PORTIA.

Well then, confess, and live.

　　BASSANIO.

　　　　　　　　　'Confess,' and 'love,'
Had been the very sum of my confession:
O happy torment, when my torturer
Doth teach me answers for deliverance!
But let me to my fortune and the caskets.

　　PORTIA.

Away, then! I am lockt in one of them:

---

[1] **peize:** this word is from the French *peser;* to peize is to weigh or balance; hence, to keep in suspense, delay. [2] **To stay you from election:** to delay your choice. [3] **rack:** torture rack. [4] **treason:** Portia speaks lightly; she does not really think him disloyal. [5] **enforced:** under compulsion.

If you do love me, you will find me out.—
Nerissa, and the rest, stand all aloof.—
Let music sound while he doth make his choice;
Then, if he lose, he makes a swan-like end,[1]
Fading in music: that the comparison
May stand more proper, my eye[2] shall be the stream
And watery death-bed for him. He may win;
And what is music then? then music is
Even as the flourish when true subjects bow
To a new-crowned monarch: such it is
As are those dulcet sounds[3] in break of day
That creep into the dreaming bridegroom's ear,
And summon him to marriage.—Now he goes,
With no less presence,[4] but with much more love,
Than young Alcides,[5] when he did redeem
The virgin tribute[6] paid by howling Troy[7]
To the sea-monster: I stand for sacrifice;[8]
The rest aloof are the Dardanian[9] wives,
With bleared visages,[10] come forth to view
The issue of th' exploit. Go, Hercules!
Live thou, I live:—with much much more dismay
I view the fight than thou that makest the fray.

Here music.—A Song, the whilst BASSANIO *comments
on the caskets to himself.*

> Tell me where is fancy bred,
> Or in the heart or in the head?
> How begot, how nourished?
>   Reply, reply.
> It is engender'd in the eyes,
> With gazing fed; and fancy dies
> In the cradle where it lies.

---

[1] **swan-like end**: die singing according to the common belief that swans sang when dying. [2] **eye**: tears. [3] **dulcet sounds**: an allusion to the custom of playing music under the bridegroom's window on the morning of his marriage. [4] **presence**: dignity of mien. [5] **Alcides**: Hercules. [6] **virgin tribute**: Hesione. [7] **howling Troy**: wailing, or lamenting, Trojans. [8] **I stand for sacrifice**: I stand here instead of Hesione. [9] **Dardanian**: Trojan. [10] **bleared visages**: tear-stained faces.

Let us all ring fancy's knell;
I'll begin it,—Ding, dong, bell.
All. Ding, dong, bell.

BASSANIO.

So may the outward shows be least themselves:[1]
The world is still deceived with ornament.
In law, what plea so tainted and corrupt,
But, being season'd with a gracious voice,
Obscures the show of evil? In religion,
What damned error, but some sober brow
Will bless it, and approve it with a text,
Hiding the grossness with fair ornament?
There is no vice so simple,[2] but assumes
Some mark of virtue on his outward parts:
How many cowards, whose hearts are all as false
As stairs of sand, wear yet upon their chins
The beards of Hercules and frowning Mars;[3]
Who, inward searcht, have livers white as milk;[4]
And these assume but valour's excrement[5]
To render them redoubted![6] Look on beauty,
And you shall see 'tis purchased by the weight;
Which therein works a miracle in nature,
Making them lightest[7] that wear most of it:
So are those crisped[8] snaky golden locks,
Which make such wanton gambols with the wind,
Upon supposed fairness, often known
To be the dowry[9] of a second head,[10]
The skull that bred them in the sepulchre.
Thus ornament is but the guiled[11] shore
To a most dangerous sea; the beauteous scarf
Veiling an Indian beauty;[12] in a word,
The seeming truth which cunning times put on

---

[1] **may outward shows be least themselves**: outward appearances may bear no relation to their intrinsic worth. [2] **simple**: trifling. [3] **beards of Hercules and frowning Mars**: i.e., manlike, brave appearance. [4] **livers white as milk**: white-livered. [5] **excrement**: in this instance, beards, a sign of virility (bravery). [6] **redoubted**: dreaded; feared. [7] **lightest**: less chaste. [8] **crisped**: curled. [9] **dowry**: possession. [10] **second head**: wig. [11] **guiled**: treacherous. [12] **Indian beauty**: not considered beautiful according to European standards.

To entrap the wisest. Therefore, thou gaudy gold,
Hard food for Midas,[1] I will none of thee;
Nor none of thee, thou stale and common drudge
'Tween man and man:[2] but thou, thou meagre[3] lead,
Which rather threatenest than dost promise aught,
Thy paleness moves me more than eloquence;
And here choose I:—joy be the consequence!

     PORTIA [*aside*].

How all the other passions fleet to air,[4]—
As doubtful thoughts, and rash-embraced[5] despair,
And shuddering fear, and green-eyed jealousy!
O love, be moderate; allay thy ecstasy;
In measure rain thy joy; scant this excess!
I feel too much thy blessing: make it less,
For fear I surfeit!

     BASSANIO.

             What find I here?

           [*Opening the leaden casket.*

Fair Portia's counterfeit![6] What demi-god
Hath come so near creation? Move these eyes?
Or whether, riding on the balls of mine,
Seem they in motion? Here are sever'd[7] lips,
Parted with sugar breath: so sweet a bar
Should sunder such sweet friends. Here in her hairs
The painter plays the spider; and hath woven
A golden mesh t'entrap the hearts of men,
Faster than gnats in cobwebs: but her eyes,—
How could he see to do them? having made one,
Methinks it should have power to steal both his,

---

[1] **Hard food for Midas:** everything, even food, that Midas touched turned to gold, and as much as he loved gold, he could not eat it. [2] **stale and common drudge/'Tween man and man:** silver was used as currency. [3] **meagre:** almost valueless as compared to gold and silver. [4] **fleet to air:** fly away. [5] **rash-embraced:** hasty. [6] **counterfeit:** portrait. [7] **sever'd:** parted.

And leave itself unfurnisht.[1] Yet look, how far
The substance of my praise doth wrong this shadow
In underprizing it, so far this shadow
Doth limp behind the substance.—Here's the scroll,
The continent[2] and summary of my fortune.

> You that choose not by the view,
> Chance as fair, and choose as true!
> Since this fortune falls to you,
> Be content, and seek no new.
> If you be well pleased with this,
> And hold your fortune for your bliss,
> Turn you where your lady is,
> And claim her with a loving kiss.

A gentle scroll.—Fair lady, by your leave;   [*Kissing her.*
I come by note, to give and to receive.
Like one of two contending in a prize,
That thinks he hath done well in people's eyes,
Hearing applause and universal shout,
Giddy in spirit, still gazing in a doubt
Whether those peals of praise be his or no;
So, thrice-fair lady, stand I, even so;
As doubtful whether what I see be true,
Until confirm'd, sign'd, ratified by you.

    PORTIA.
You see me, Lord Bassanio, where I stand,
Such as I am: though for myself alone

---

[1] unfurnisht: unpainted because the artist cannot see to complete
the painting.
[2] The continent: that which contains; equivalent to "summary."

I would not be ambitious in my wish,
To wish myself much better; yet for you
I would be trebled twenty times myself;
A thousand times more fair, ten thousand times more rich;
That, only to stand high in your account,
I might in virtues, beauties, livings, friends,
Exceed account: but the full sum of me
Is sum of nothing; which, to term in gross,[1]
Is an unlesson'd girl, unschool'd, unpractised:
Happy in this, she is not yet so old
But she may learn; happier than this,
She is not bred so dull but she can learn;
Happiest of all is that her gentle spirit
Commits itself to yours to be directed,
As from her lord, her governor, her king.
Myself and what is mine to you and yours
Is now converted: but now I was the lord
Of this fair mansion, master of my servants,
Queen o'er myself; and even now, but now,
This house, these servants, and this same myself,
Are yours, my lord: I give them with this ring;
Which when you part from, lose, or give away,
Let it presage the ruin of your love,
And be my vantage to exclaim on you.[2]

BASSANIO.

Madam, you have bereft me of all words,
Only my blood speaks to you in my veins:
And there is such confusion in my powers,
As, after some oration fairly spoke
By a beloved prince, there doth appear
Among the buzzing pleased multitude;

---

[1] term in gross: mention its full amount.
[2] be my vantage to exclaim on you: be my opportunity to cry out
against you.

Where every something, being blent together,
Turns to a wild of nothing,[1] save of joy,
Exprest and not exprest. But when this ring
Parts from this finger, then parts life from hence:
O, then be bold to say Bassanio's dead!

NERISSA.

My lord and lady, it is now our time,
That have stood by, and seen our wishes prosper,
To cry, good joy:—good joy, my lord and lady!

GRATIANO.

My Lord Bassanio and my gentle lady,
I wish you all the joy that you can wish;
For I am sure you can wish none from me:
And, when your honours mean to solemnize
The bargain of your faith, I do beseech you,
Even at that time I may be married too.

BASSANIO.

With all my heart, so thou canst get a wife.

GRATIANO.

I thank your lordship, you have got me one.
My eyes, my lord, can look as swift as yours:
You saw the mistress, I beheld the maid;
You loved, I loved; for intermission[2]
No more pertains to me, my lord, than you.
Your fortune stood upon the caskets there;
And so did mine too, as the matter falls;
For wooing here, until I sweat again,
And swearing, till my very roof [3] was dry
With oaths of love, at last,—if promise last,[4]—
I got a promise of this fair one here,
To have her love, provided that your fortune
Achieved her mistress.

---

[1] wild of nothing: chaos.
[2] for intermission: to occupy their leisure time.
[3] roof: roof of his mouth.
[4] if promise last: if her promise remain good.

PORTIA.

Is this true, Nerissa?

NERISSA.

Madam, it is, so you stand pleased withal.

BASSANIO.

And do you, Gratiano, mean good faith?

GRATIANO.

Yes, faith, my lord.

BASSANIO.

Our feast shall be much honour'd in your marriage.

GRATIANO.

We'll play[1] with them the first boy for a thousand ducats.

NERISSA.

What, and stake down? [2]

GRATIANO.

No; we shall ne'er win at that sport, and stake down.—
But who comes here? Lorenzo and his infidel?
What, and my old Venetian friend Solanio?

Enter LORENZO, JESSICA, *and* SOLANIO.

BASSANIO.

Lorenzo and Solanio, welcome hither;
If that the youth of my new interest here[3]
Have power to bid you welcome.—By your leave,
I bid my very friends and countrymen,
Sweet Portia, welcome.

PORTIA.

So do I, my lord;
They are entirely welcome.

---

[1] play: wager.
[2] and stake down: and lay down the stakes.
[3] youth of my new interest here: his newly acquired prerogative to give orders here.

LORENZO.

I thank your honour.—For my part, my lord,
My purpose was not to have seen you here;
But meeting with Solanio by the way,
He did entreat me, past all saying nay,
To come with him along.

SOLANIO.

              I did, my lord;
And I have reason for't. Signior Antonio
Commends him to you.   [*Gives* BASSANIO *a letter.*

BASSANIO.

            Ere I ope his letter,
I pray you, tell me how my good friend doth.

SOLANIO.

Not sick, my lord, unless it be in mind;
Not well, unless in mind: his letter there
Will show you his estate.   [BASSANIO *reads the letter.*

GRATIANO.

Nerissa, cheer yon stranger; bid her welcome.—
Your hand, Solanio: what's the news from Venice?
How doth that royal merchant, good Antonio?
I know he will be glad of our success;
We are the Jasons,[1] we have won the fleece.

SOLANIO.

I would you had won the fleece that he hath lost!

PORTIA.

There are some shrewd [2] contents in yon same paper,
That steals the colour from Bassanio's cheek:
Some dear friend dead; else nothing in the world

---

[1] Jasons: an allusion to Jason, the Greek hero who sailed to Colchis
in search of the Golden Fleece.
[2] shrewd: distressing.

Could turn so much the constitution[1]
Of any constant[2] man. What, worse and worse!—
With leave, Bassanio; I am half yourself,
And I must freely have the half of any thing
That this same paper brings you.

BASSANIO.

O sweet Portia,
Here are a few of the unpleasant'st words
That ever blotted paper! Gentle lady,
When I did first impart my love to you,
I freely told you, all the wealth I had
Ran in my veins,—I was a gentleman;
An   I told you true: and yet, dear lady,
Rating myself at nothing, you shall see
How much I was a braggart. When I told you
My state was nothing, I should then have told you
That I was worse than nothing; for, indeed,
I have engaged [3] myself to a dear friend,
Engaged my friend to his mere[4] enemy,
To feed my means. Here is a letter, lady,—
The paper as the body of my friend,
And every word in it a gaping wound,
Issuing life-blood.—But is it true, Solanio?
Have all his ventures fail'd? What, not one hit? [5]
From Tripolis, from Mexico, and England,
From Lisbon, Barbary, and India?
And not one vessel scape[6] the dreadful touch
Of merchant-marring rocks?

SOLANIO.

Not one, my lord.
Besides, it should appear, that if he had
The present[7] money to discharge[8] the Jew,

---

[1] **constitution:** innate nature. [2] **constant:** self-contained. [3] **engaged:** pledged. [4] **mere:** unqualified; out-and-out. [5] **hit:** success. [6] **scape:** escaped. [7] **present:** available. [8] **discharge:** discharge his obligation to.

He would not take it. Never did I know
A creature, that did bear the shape of man,
So keen and greedy to confound [1] a man;
He plies the duke at morning and at night;
And doth impeach the freedom of the state,[2]
If they deny him justice: twenty merchants,
The duke himself, and the magnificoes[3]
Of greatest port,[4] have all persuaded with him;[5]
But none can drive him from the envious[6] plea
Of forfeiture, of justice, and his bond.

JESSICA.

When I was with him, I have heard him swear,
To Tubal and to Chus, his countrymen,
That he would rather have Antonio's flesh
Than twenty times the value of the sum
That he did owe him: and I know, my lord,
If law, authority, and power deny not,
It will go hard with poor Antonio.

PORTIA.

Is it your dear friend that is thus in trouble?

BASSANIO.

The dearest friend to me, the kindest man,
The best-condition'd and unwearied spirit
In doing courtesies; and one in whom
The ancient Roman honour more appears
Than any that draws breath in Italy.

PORTIA.

What sum owes he the Jew?

BASSANIO.

For me three thousand ducats.

PORTIA.

What, no more?
Pay him six thousand, and deface[7] the bond;

---

[1] confound: ruin. [2] doth impeach the freedom of the state: accuses
the state of not guaranteeing the rights of its citizens. [3] magnificoes:
highest nobles. [4] port: bearing; dignity. [5] persuaded with him:
tried to reason with him. [6] envious: malicious. [7] deface: destroy.

Double six thousand, and then treble that,
Before a friend of this description
Shall lose a hair through Bassanio's fault.
First go with me to church and call me wife,
And then away to Venice to your friend;
For never shall you lie by Portia's side
With an unquiet soul. You shall have gold
To pay the petty debt twenty times over:
When it is paid, bring your true friend along.
My maid Nerissa and myself meantime
Will live as maids and widows.[1] Come, away!
For you shall hence upon your wedding-day:
Bid your friends welcome, show a merry cheer:
Since you are dear-bought, I will love you dear.—
But let me hear the letter of your friend.

BASSANIO [reads].

Sweet Bassanio, my ships have all miscarried,[2] my creditors grow cruel, my estate is very low, my bond to the Jew is forfeit; and since in paying it, it is impossible I should live, all debts are clear'd between you and I, if I might but see you at my death. Notwithstanding, use your pleasure: if your love do not persuade you to come, let not my letter.

PORTIA.

O love, dispatch all business, and be gone!

BASSANIO.

Since I have your good leave to go away,
    I will make haste: but, till I come again,
No bed shall e'er be guilty of my stay,
    No rest be interposer 'twixt us twain.   [Exeunt.

---

[1] Will live as maids and widows: will be true to you and lament your absence.
[2] have all miscarried: have all been lost.

SCENE III.

Venice. A street.

Enter SHYLOCK, SALARINO, ANTONIO, *and* GAOLER.

SHYLOCK.

Gaoler, look to him:—tell not me of mercy;—
This is the fool that lent out money gratis:—
Gaoler, look to him.

ANTONIO.

Hear me yet, good Shylock.

SHYLOCK.

I'll have my bond; speak not against my bond:
I have sworn an oath that I will have my bond.
Thou call'dst me dog before thou hadst a cause;
But, since I am a dog, beware my fangs:
The duke shall grant me justice.—I do wonder,
Thou naughty[1] gaoler, that thou art so fond [2]
To come abroad [3] with him at his request.

ANTONIO.

I pray thee, hear me speak.

SHYLOCK.

I'll have my bond; I will not hear thee speak:
I'll have my bond; and therefore speak no more.
I'll not be made a soft and dull-eyed fool,
To shake the head, relent, and sigh, and yield
To Christian intercessors. Follow not;
I'll have no speaking: I will have my bond.   [*Exit.*

SALARINO.

It is the most impenetrable cur
That ever kept with[4] men.

---

[1] naughty: wicked.
[2] fond: foolish.
[3] to come abroad: to let him walk out with his friends.
[4] kept with: resided with; lived with.

ANTONIO.

Let him alone:
I'll follow him no more with bootless[1] prayers.
He seeks my life; his reason well I know:
I oft deliver'd from his forfeitures
Many that have at times made moan to me;[2]
Therefore he hates me.

SALARINO.

I am sure the duke
Will never grant this forfeiture to hold.

ANTONIO.

The duke cannot deny the course of law;
For the commodity[3] that strangers have
With us in Venice, if it be denied,
Will much impeach the justice of the state;
Since that the trade and profit of the city
Consisteth of all nations. Therefore, go:
These griefs and losses have so bated[4] me,
That I shall hardly spare a pound of flesh
To-morrow to my bloody creditor.—
Well, gaoler, on.—Pray God, Bassanio come
To see me pay his debt,—and then I care not!   [*Exeunt.*

SCENE IV.

Belmont. A room in PORTIA's *house.*

Enter PORTIA, NERISSA, LORENZO, JESSICA,
and BALTHAZAR, *a man of* PORTIA's.

LORENZO.

Madam, although I speak it in your presence,
You have a noble and a true conceit[5]
Of god-like amity,[6] which appears most strongly
In bearing thus the absence of your lord.

---

[1] bootless: unavailing; useless.
[2] made moan to me: begged me for assistance.
[3] commodity: favorable trade relations.
[4] bated: reduced.
[5] conceit: understanding; conception.
[6] amity: friendship.

But if you knew to whom you show this honour,
How true a gentleman you send relief,
How dear a lover of my lord your husband,
I know you would be prouder of the work
Than customary bounty can enforce you.[1]

PORTIA.

I never did repent for doing good,
Nor shall not now: for in companions
That do converse and waste[2] the time together,
Whose souls do bear an egal yoke[3] of love,
There must be needs a like proportion
Of lineaments, of manners, and of spirit;
Which makes me think that this Antonio,
Being the bosom lover[4] of my lord,
Must needs be like my lord. If it be so,
How little is the cost I have bestow'd
In purchasing the semblance of my soul [5]
From out the state of hellish cruelty!
This comes too near the praising of myself;
Therefore no more of it: hear other things.—
Lorenzo, I commit into your hands
The husbandry and manage of my house
Until my lord's return: for mine own part,
I have toward heaven breathed a secret vow
To live in prayer and contemplation,
Only attended by Nerissa here,
Until her husband and my lord's return:
There is a monastery two miles off;
And there will we abide. I do desire you
Not to deny this imposition;
The which my love and some necessity
Now lays upon you.

---

[1] Than customary bounty can enforce you: it would give you greater satisfaction than any ordinary good deed could.
[2] waste: spend.
[3] egal yoke: equal burden.
[4] lover: friend.
[5] semblance of my soul: one who is like Bassanio, whom I love as my own soul.

LORENZO.
                    Madam, with all my heart;
I shall obey you in all fair commands.

PORTIA.
My people do already know my mind,
And will acknowledge you and Jessica
In place of Lord Bassanio and myself.
So fare you well, till we shall meet again.

LORENZO.
Fair thoughts and happy hours attend on you!

JESSICA.
I wish your ladyship all heart's content.

PORTIA.
I thank you for your wish, and am well pleased
To wish it back on you: fare you well, Jessica.

                    [*Exeunt* JESSICA *and* LORENZO.

Now, Balthazar,
As I have ever found thee honest-true,[1]
So let me find thee still. Take this same letter,
And use thou all the endeavour of a man
In speed to Padua: see thou render[2] this
Into my cousin's hand, Doctor Bellario;
And, look, what notes and garments he doth give thee,
Bring them, I pray thee, with imagined speed [3]
Unto the tranect,[4] to the common ferry
Which trades to Venice. Waste no time in words,
But get thee gone: I shall be there before thee.

BALTHAZAR.
Madam, I go with all convenient speed.   [*Exit.*

PORTIA.
Come on, Nerissa; I have work in hand

---

[1] **honest-true:** honorable and trustworthy.
[2] **render:** deliver.
[3] **imagined speed:** the speed of thought.
[4] **tranect:** the ferry between Venice and the mainland.

That you yet know not of: we'll see our husbands
Before they think of us.

NERISSA.

Shall they see us?

PORTIA.

They shall, Nerissa; but in such a habit,
That they shall think we are accomplished [1]
With that we lack.[2] I'll hold thee any wager,
When we are both accoutred like young men,
I'll prove the prettier fellow of the two,
And wear my dagger with the braver grace;
And speak between the change of man and boy,
With a reed voice; and turn two mincing steps
Into a manly stride; and speak of frays,[3]
Like a fine-bragging youth; and tell quaint[4] lies,
How honourable ladies sought my love,
Which I denying, they fell sick and died,—
I could not do withal;—then I'll repent,
And wish, for all that, that I had not kill'd them:
And twenty of these puny lies I'll tell;
That men shall swear I have discontinued school
Above a twelvemonth:[5]—I have within my mind
A thousand raw tricks of these bragging Jacks,[6]
Which I will practise.

NERISSA.

Why, shall we turn to men?

PORTIA.

Fie, what a question's that,
If thou wert near a lewd interpreter!
But come, I'll tell thee all my whole device[7]
When I am in my coach, which stays for us
At the park-gate; and therefore haste away,
For we must measure twenty miles to-day.   [*Exeunt.*

---

[1] **accomplished**: furnished. [2] **With that we lack**: that is, they shall
take the two for men. [3] **frays**: brawls. [4] **quaint**: elaborate; clever.
[5] **above a twelvemonth**: over a year. [6] **bragging Jacks**: boasting
fellows. [7] **device**: plan.

SCENE V.

The same. A garden.

Enter LAUNCELOT and JESSICA.

LAUNCELOT.

Yes, truly; for, look you, the sins of the father are to be laid upon the children: therefore, I promise ye, I fear you.[1] I was always plain with you, and so now I speak my agitation[2] of the matter: therefore be o' good cheer; for, truly, I think you are damn'd. There is but one hope in it that can do you any good; and that is but a kind of bastard hope neither.

JESSICA.

And what hope is that, I pray thee?

LAUNCELOT.

Marry, you may partly hope that your father got you not,—that you are not the Jew's daughter.

JESSICA.

That were a kind of bastard hope, indeed: so the sins of my mother should be visited upon me.

LAUNCELOT.

Truly, then, I fear you are damn'd both by father and mother: thus when I shun Scylla,[3] your father, I fall into Charybdis,[4] your mother: well, you are gone both ways.

JESSICA.

I shall be saved by my husband; he hath made me a Christian.

LAUNCELOT.

Truly, the more to blame he: we were Christians enow before;[5] e'en as many as could well live, one by another. This

---

[1] I fear you: I fear for you. [2] agitation: cogitation; opinion. [3] Scylla: a rock on the Italian coast opposite the whirlpool Charybdis, both menaces to seafarers. [4] Charybdis: see above. [5] we were Christians enow be/fore: there were enough Christians in the world before this.

making of Christians will raise the price of hogs: if we grow all to be pork-eaters, we shall not shortly have a rasher on the coals for money.

JESSICA.

I'll tell my husband, Launcelot, what you say: here he comes.

Enter LORENZO.

LORENZO.

I shall grow jealous of you shortly, Launcelot, if you thus get my wife into corners.

JESSICA.

Nay, you need not fear us, Lorenzo: Launcelot and I are out.[1] He tells me flatly, there's no mercy for me in heaven, because I am a Jew's daughter: and he says, you are no good member of the commonwealth; for, in converting Jews to Christians, you raise the price of pork.

LORENZO.

I shall answer that better to the commonwealth than you can the getting up of the negro's belly: the Moor's with child by you, Launcelot.

LAUNCELOT.

It is much that the Moor should be more than reason:[2] but if she be less than an honest woman, she is indeed more than I took her for.

LORENZO.

How every fool can play upon the word! I think the best grace of wit will shortly turn into silence, and discourse grow commendable in none only but parrots.—Go in, sirrah; bid them prepare for dinner.

---

[1] **are out**: have fallen out; quarreled.
[2] **more than reason**: more than is reasonable; chaste.

LAUNCELOT.

That's done, sir; they have all stomachs.[1]

LORENZO.

Goodly Lord, what a wit-snapper are you! then bid them prepare dinner.

LAUNCELOT.

That is done too, sir; only 'cover' [2] is the word.

LORENZO.

Will you cover, then, sir?

LAUNCELOT.

Not so, sir, neither; I know my duty.

LORENZO.

Yet more quarrelling with occasion! [3] Wilt thou show the
whole wealth of thy wit in an instant? I pray thee, understand a plain man in his plain meaning: go to thy fellows,
bid them cover the table, serve in the meat, and we will come
in to dinner.

LAUNCELOT.

For the table, sir, it shall be served in; for the meat, sir, it
shall be cover'd; for your coming in to dinner, sir, why, let it
be as humours and conceits shall govern.   [Exit.

LORENZO.

O dear discretion, how his words are suited! [4]
The fool hath planted in his memory
An army of good words; and I do know
A many fools, that stand in better place,
Garnisht like him, that for a tricksy[5] word
Defy the matter.—How cheer'st thou, Jessica?
And now, good sweet, say thy opinion,—
How dost thou like the Lord Bassanio's wife?

---

[1] stomachs: appetites. [2] "cover": Launcelot means that Lorenzo
should have said "set the table." [3] quarreling with occasion: quib-
bling or making perverse remarks at every opportunity. [4] suited:
matched to suit a perverted meaning. [5] tricksy: fantastically dressed
up, with no regard for the subject under discussion.

JESSICA.

Past all expressing. It is very meet[1]
The Lord Bassanio live an upright life;
For, having such a blessing in his lady,
He finds the joys of heaven here on earth;
And if on earth he do not mean[2] it, then
In reason he should never come to heaven.
Why, if two gods should play some heavenly match,
And on the wager lay two earthly women,
And Portia one, there must be something else
Pawn'd [3] with the other; for the poor rude world
Hath not her fellow.[4]

LORENZO.

            Even such a husband
Hast thou of me as she is for a wife.

JESSICA.

Nay, but ask my opinion too of that.

LORENZO.

I will anon: first, let us go to dinner.

JESSICA.

Nay, let me praise you while I have a stomach.[5]

LORENZO.

No, prithee, let it serve for table-talk;
Then, howsoe'er thou speak'st, 'mong other things
I shall digest it.

JESSICA.

        Well, I'll set you forth.[6]   [*Exeunt.*

---

[1] meet: proper; fitting.
[2] mean: probably should be "merit."
[3] Pawn'd: added; staked.
[4] fellow: equal.
[5] stomach: desire for it.
[6] set you forth: praise you extravagantly.

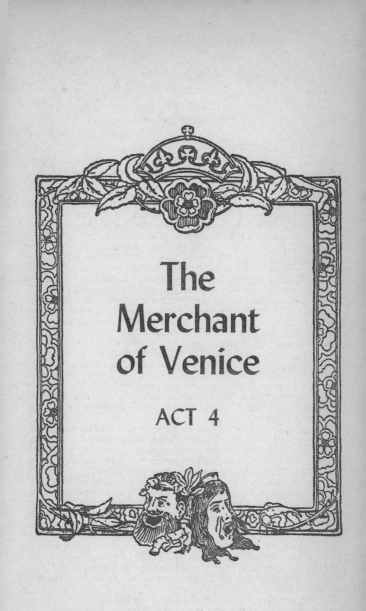

The
Merchant
of Venice

ACT 4

ACT IV

THE TRIAL begins in Venice. The Duke pleads with Shylock not only to show mercy toward Antonio but to forgive him half the principal of the debt. Shylock answers that he intends to have the law. Bassanio offers him six thousand ducats. Shylock replies that, according to the laws of Venice, he has the right to a pound of Antonio's flesh. The Duke threatens to dismiss the court unless Bellario comes; he is informed by Salarino that a messenger has arrived with letters from the doctor. While Nerissa presents a letter to the Duke, Gratiano damns Shylock, who is whetting a knife on the sole of his boot. The Duke announces that the letter commends a learned young doctor to the court; he reads the letter and Portia, disguised as a doctor of laws, enters. She asks that the merchant and the Jew be presented to her, and then tells Shylock that he must be merciful because mercy is the true prerogative of power and indeed a divine attribute. Shylock demands only justice. Bassanio informs Portia that he has more than enough money to pay the bond and pleads with the Duke to bend the law a little to save Antonio's life. Portia refuses to consider this, thus arousing Shylock's highest admiration. She tells him that thrice his money is offered to him, but Shylock refuses, saying he has sworn an oath. Portia tells Antonio to prepare for the knife and asks Shylock to provide a surgeon so that Antonio will not bleed to death. Shylock refuses. Antonio gives Bassanio a last farewell, and Bassanio and Gratiano vow that they would sacrifice both themselves and their wives for his life.

Shylock is about to cut when Portia interrupts him by saying the bond gives him no drop of blood; that if Shylock sheds one drop, his lands and goods will be confiscated by the state of Venice. Shylock, thwarted, demands the offer of thrice the bond, only to have Portia interrupt him with another legal setback. If he cuts more or less than exactly one pound, he will die and all his goods will be confiscated. Shylock then demands the bare principal; when this is refused, he attempts to leave. Portia stops him. She tells him that because he, an alien, has conspired against the life of a Venetian, his own life is at the mercy of the Duke, half his goods shall go to the state and the other half to Antonio. The Duke pardons Shylock's life and reduces the public penalty against his estate to a fine; Antonio offers to hold his half of Shylock's goods for Lorenzo, on condition that Shylock become a Christian and that he make a will giving all his goods at his death to his daughter and son-in-law.

For her services Portia will take nothing but Bassanio's gloves and his ring. Bassanio at first refuses her the ring, then relents and sends it after her by Gratiano, who gives her Bassanio's ring and Nerissa his own.

ACT IV. Scene I.

Venice. A court of justice.

Enter the DUKE, *the* MAGNIFICOES, ANTONIO, BASSANIO, GRATIANO, SOLANIO, SALARINO, *and others.*

DUKE OF VENICE.
What, is Antonio here?

ANTONIO.
Ready,[1] so please your Grace.

DUKE OF VENICE.
I am sorry for thee: thou art come to answer
A stony adversary, an inhuman wretch
Uncapable of pity; void and empty
From[2] any dram[3] of mercy.

ANTONIO.
                      I have heard
Your Grace hath ta'en great pains to qualify[4]
His rigorous course; but since he stands obdurate,
And that no lawful means can carry me
Out of his envy's reach, I do oppose
My patience to his fury; and am arm'd
To suffer, with a quietness of spirit,
The very tyranny and rage of his.

DUKE OF VENICE.
Go one, and call the Jew into the court.

SOLANIO.
He's ready at the door: he comes, my lord.

Enter SHYLOCK.

DUKE OF VENICE.
Make room, and let him stand before our face.—
Shylock, the world thinks, and I think so too,
That thou but lead'st this fashion of thy malice[5]

---

[1] Ready: the standard answer in court.
[2] From: of.
[3] dram: minute quantity; drop.
[4] qualify: moderate; soften.
[5] lead'st this fashion of thy malice: pretend to carry through this spiteful action.

To the last hour of act; and then 'tis thought
Thou'lt show thy mercy and remorse[1] more strange
Than is thy strange apparent cruelty;
And where thou now exact'st the penalty,—
Which is a pound of this poor merchant's flesh,—
Thou wilt not only loose[2] the forfeiture,
But, toucht with human gentleness and love,
Forgive a moiety[3] of the principal;
Glancing an eye of pity on his losses,
That have of late so huddled on his back,
Enow[4] to press a royal merchant[5] down,
And pluck commiseration of his state
From brassy bosoms and rough hearts of flint,
From stubborn Turks and Tartars, never train'd
To offices of tender courtesy.
We all expect a gentle answer, Jew.

SHYLOCK.

I have possest[6] your Grace of what I purpose;
And by our holy Sabbath have I sworn
To have the due and forfeit[7] of my bond:
If you deny it, let the danger light
Upon your charter and your city's freedom.
You'll ask me, why I rather choose to have
A weight of carrion-flesh than to receive
Three thousand ducats: I'll not answer that;
But say it is my humour: is it answer'd?
What if my house be troubled with a rat,
And I be pleased to give ten thousand ducats
To have it baned! [8] What, are you answer'd yet?
Some men there are love not a gaping pig;[9]
Some, that are mad if they behold a cat;[10]

---

[1] remorse: pity; compassion. [2] loose: release. [3] moiety: part; portion.
[4] Enow: enough. [5] royal merchant: a merchant with the resources
of the kingdom behind him. [6] possest: informed. [7] due and forfeit:
the forfeit which is due. [8] baned: poisoned. [9] a gaping pig: a suck-
ling pig served at the table with a lemon or some other fruit in
its mouth. [10] behold a cat: some people have a natural antipathy
to cats.

And others, when the bag-pipe sings i' th' nose,
Cannot contain their urine: for affection,[1]
Mistress of passion, sways it to the mood
Of what it likes or loathes. Now, for your answer:
As there is no firm reason to be render'd,
Why he cannot abide a gaping pig;
Why he, a harmless necessary cat;
Why he, a woollen bag-pipe,—but of force
Must yield to such inevitable shame
As to offend himself, being offended;
So can I give no reason, nor I will not,
More than a lodged [2] hate and a certain[3] loathing
I bear Antonio, that I follow thus
A losing suit against him. Are you answer'd?

> BASSANIO.

This is no answer, thou unfeeling man,
To excuse the current[4] of thy cruelty.

> SHYLOCK.

I am not bound to please thee with my answer.

> BASSANIO.

Do all men kill the things they do not love?

> SHYLOCK.

Hates any man the thing he would not kill?

> BASSANIO.

Every offence is not a hate at first.

> SHYLOCK.

What, would'st thou have a serpent sting thee twice?

> ANTONIO.

I pray you, think you question with the Jew:
You may as well go stand upon the beach,
And bid the main flood [5] bate[6] his usual height;

---

[1] affection: sympathetic feeling; one's likes and dislikes.
[2] lodged: deep-seated.
[3] certain: sure; fixed.
[4] current: course.
[5] main flood: ocean.
[6] bate: abate.

You may as well use question with the wolf,
Why he hath made the ewe bleat for the lamb;
You may as well forbid the mountain pines
To wag their high tops, and to make no noise,
When they are fretten with the gusts of heaven;[1]
You may as well do any thing most hard,
As seek to soften that,—than which what's harder?—
His Jewish heart:—therefore, I do beseech you,
Make no more offers, use no further means,
But, with all brief and plain conveniency,[2]
Let me have judgement, and the Jew his will.

BASSANIO.

For thy three thousand ducats here is six.

SHYLOCK.

If every ducat in six thousand ducats
Were in six parts, and every part a ducat,
I would not draw[3] them,—I would have my bond.

DUKE OF VENICE.

How shalt thou hope for mercy, rendering none?

SHYLOCK.

What judgement shall I dread, doing no wrong?
You have among you many a purchased slave,
Which, like your asses and your dogs and mules,
You use in abject and in slavish parts[4]
Because you bought them:—shall I say to you,
Let them be free, marry them to your heirs?
Why sweat they under burdens? let their beds
Be made as soft as yours, and let their palates
Be season'd with such viands? You will answer,
The slaves are ours:—so do I answer you:
The pound of flesh, which I demand of him,

---

[1] fretten with the gusts of heaven: ruffled or tossed by high winds.
[2] plain conveniency: simple procedure.
[3] draw: take.
[4] parts: services; tasks.

Is dearly bought, 'tis mine, and I will have it.
If you deny me, fie upon your law!
There is no force in the decrees of Venice.
I stand for judgement: answer,—shall I have it?

DUKE OF VENICE.

Upon my power I may dismiss this court,
Unless Bellario, a learned doctor,
Whom I have sent for to determine this,
Come here to-day.

SOLANIO.

                    My lord, here stays without
A messenger with letters from the doctor,
New come from Padua.

DUKE OF VENICE.

Bring us the letters; call the messenger.

BASSANIO.

Good cheer, Antonio! What, man, courage yet
The Jew shall have my flesh, blood, bones, and all,
Ere thou shalt lose for me one drop of blood.

ANTONIO.

I am a tainted wether[1] of the flock,
Meetest[2] for death: the weakest kind of fruit
Drops earliest to the ground; and so let me:
You cannot better be employ'd, Bassanio,
Than to live still, and write mine epitaph.

Enter NERISSA, *dressed like a lawyer's clerk.*

DUKE OF VENICE.

Came you from Padua, from Bellario?

NERISSA.

From both, my lord. Bellario greets your Grace.
                              [*Presents a letter.*

---

[1] wether: gelded sheep.
[2] Meetest: most fit.

BASSANIO.

Why dost thou whet thy knife so earnestly?

SHYLOCK.

To cut the forfeiture from that bankrout[1] there.

GRATIANO.

Not on thy sole, but on thy soul, harsh Jew,
Thou makest thy knife keen; but no metal can,
No, not the hangman's axe, bear half the keenness
Of thy sharp envy. Can no prayers pierce thee?

SHYLOCK.

No, none that thou hast wit enough to make.

GRATIANO.

O, be thou damn'd, inexecrable[2] dog!
And for thy life let justice be accused.
Thou almost makest me waver in my faith,
To hold opinion[3] with Pythagoras,
That souls of animals infuse themselves
Into the trunks of men: thy currish spirit
Govern'd a wolf, who, hang'd for human slaughter,
Even from the gallows did his fell [4] soul fleet,
And, whilst thou lay'st in thy unhallow'd dam,
Infused itself in thee; for thy desires
Are wolvish, bloody, starved, and ravenous.

SHYLOCK.

Till thou canst rail the seal from off my bond,
Thou but offend'st thy lungs to speak so loud:
Repair thy wit, good youth, or it will fall
To cureless ruin.[5]—I stand here for law.

DUKE OF VENICE.

This letter from Bellario doth commend
A young and learned doctor to our court.—
Where is he?

---

[1] bankrout: bankrupt.
[2] inexecrable: so execrable, or evil, that you are beyond enough cursing.
[3] To hold opinion with: to agree with.
[4] fell: cruel; deadly.
[5] cureless ruin: insanity.

NERISSA.

He attendeth here hard by,[1]
To know your answer, whether you'll admit him.

DUKE OF VENICE.

With all my heart.—Some three or four of you
Go give him courteous conduct to this place.—
Meantime the court shall hear Bellario's letter.

CLERK [reads].

Your Grace shall understand, that at the receipt of your letter
I am very sick: but in the instant that your messenger came,
in loving visitation[2] was with me a young doctor of Rome;
his name is Balthazar. I acquainted him with the cause in
controversy between the Jew and Antonio the merchant: we
turn'd o'er many books together: he is furnisht with my opinion; which, better'd with his own learning,—the greatness
whereof I cannot enough commend,—comes with him, at my
importunity, to fill up[3] your Grace's request in my stead. I
beseech you, let his lack of years be no impediment to let
him lack a reverend estimation;[4] for I never knew so young a
body with so old a head. I leave him to your gracious ac-
ceptance, whose trial shall better publish his commendation.[5]

DUKE OF VENICE.

You hear the learn'd Bellario, what he writes:
And here, I take it, is the doctor come.

Enter PORTIA *for* BALTHAZAR.

Give me your hand. Come you from old Bellario?

PORTIA.

I did, my lord.

---

[1] hard by: near by.
[2] in loving visitation: on a friendly visit.
[3] to fill up: to comply with.
[4] reverend estimation: thoughtful consideration.
[5] whose trial shall better publish his commendation: his performance will prove his ability better than I can describe it.

DUKE OF VENICE.

     You are welcome: take your place.
Are you acquainted with the difference
That holds this present question in the court?

PORTIA.

I am informed throughly[1] of the cause.—
Which is the merchant here, and which the Jew?

DUKE OF VENICE.

Antonio and old Shylock, both stand forth.

PORTIA.

Is your name Shylock?

SHYLOCK.

     Shylock is my name.

PORTIA.

Of a strange nature is the suit you follow;
Yet in such rule,[2] that the Venetian law
Cannot impugn you as you do proceed.—
You stand within his danger,[3] do you not?

ANTONIO.

Ay, so he says.

PORTIA.

    Do you confess the bond?

ANTONIO.

I do.

PORTIA.

 Then must the Jew be merciful.

SHYLOCK.

On what compulsion must I? tell me that.

PORTIA.

The quality of mercy is not strain'd,[4]—
It droppeth as the gentle rain from heaven

---

[1] throughly: thoroughly.
[2] in such rule: so much within the rules.
[3] danger: reach or control.
[4] strain'd: restricted to a few persons.

Upon the place beneath: it is twice blest,—
It blesseth him that gives, and him that takes:
'Tis mightiest in the mightiest: it becomes
The throned monarch better than his crown;
His sceptre shows the force of temporal power,
The attribute to awe and majesty,
Wherein doth sit the dread and fear of kings;
But mercy is above this sceptred sway,—
It is enthroned in the hearts of kings,
It is an attribute to God himself;
And earthly power doth then show likest God's
When mercy seasons justice. Therefore, Jew,
Though justice[1] be thy plea, consider this,—
That, in the course of justice, none of us
Should see salvation: we do pray for mercy;
And that same prayer[2] doth teach us all to render
The deeds of mercy. I have spoke thus much
To mitigate the justice of thy plea;[3]
Which if thou follow, this strict court of Venice
Must needs give sentence 'gainst the merchant there.

SHYLOCK.

My deeds upon my head! I crave the law,
The penalty and forfeit of my bond.

PORTIA.

Is he not able to discharge the money?

BASSANIO.

Yes, here I tender it for him in the court;
Yea, thrice the sum: if that will not suffice,
I will be bound to pay it ten times o'er,
On forfeit of my hands, my head, my heart:
If this will not suffice, it must appear

---

[1] justice: Shylock's plea was judgment, not justice.
[2] that same prayer: the Lord's Prayer.
[3] mitigate the justice of thy plea: temper your insistence on strict justice.

That malice bears down truth. And I beseech you,
Wrest[1] once the law to your authority:
To do a great right, do a little wrong;
And curb this cruel devil of his will.

PORTIA.

It must not be; there is no power in Venice
Can alter a decree established:
'Twill be recorded for a precedent;
And many an error, by the same example,
Will rush into the state: it cannot be.

SHYLOCK.

A Daniel[2] come to judgement! yea, a Daniel!—
O wise young judge, how I do honour thee!

PORTIA.

I pray you, let me look upon the bond.

SHYLOCK.

Here 'tis, most reverend doctor, here it is.

PORTIA.

Shylock, there's thrice thy money offer'd thee.

SHYLOCK.

An oath, an oath, I have an oath in heaven:
Shall I lay perjury upon my soul?
No, not for Venice.

PORTIA.

Why, this bond is forfeit;
And lawfully by this the Jew may claim
A pound of flesh, to be by him cut off
Nearest the merchant's heart.—Be merciful:
Take thrice thy money; bid me tear the bond.

SHYLOCK.

When it is paid according to the tenour.—
It doth appear you are a worthy judge;

---

[1] wrest: bend.
[2] Daniel: a Biblical reference to Daniel convicting the elders for spying on Susannah.

You know the law, your exposition
Hath been most sound: I charge you by the law,
Whereof you are a well-deserving pillar,
Proceed to judgement: by my soul I swear
There is no power in the tongue of man
To alter me: I stay here on my bond.

ANTONIO.

Most heartily I do beseech the court
To give the judgement.

PORTIA.

                      Why then, thus it is:—
You must prepare your bosom for his knife.

SHYLOCK.

O noble judge! O excellent young man!

PORTIA.

For the intent and purpose of the law
Hath full relation to the penalty,[1]
Which here appeareth due upon the bond.

SHYLOCK.

'Tis very true: O wise and upright judge!
How much more elder[2] art thou than thy looks!

PORTIA.

Therefore lay bare your bosom.

SHYLOCK.

                              Ay, his breast:
So says the bond:—doth it not, noble judge?—
Nearest his heart: those are the very words.

PORTIA.

It is so. Are there balance here to weigh
The flesh?

SHYLOCK.

I have them ready.

---

[1] Hath full relation to the penalty: fully recognizes the validity of the penalty.
[2] more elder: wiser in years.

PORTIA.

Have by some surgeon, Shylock, on your charge,[1]
To stop his wounds, lest he do bleed to death.

SHYLOCK.

Is it so nominated in the bond?

PORTIA.

It is not so exprest: but what of that?
'Twere good you do so much for charity.

SHYLOCK.

I cannot find it; 'tis not in the bond.

PORTIA.

You, merchant, have you any thing to say?

ANTONIO.

But little: I am arm'd and well prepared.—
Give me your hand, Bassanio: fare you well!
Grieve not that I am fall'n to this for you;
For herein Fortune shows herself more kind
Than is her custom: it is still her use
To let the wretched man outlive his wealth,
To view with hollow eye and wrinkled brow
An age of poverty; from which lingering penance
Of such a misery doth she cut me off.
Commend me to your honourable wife:
Tell her the process of Antonio's end;
Say how I loved you, speak me fair in death;
And, when the tale is told, bid her be judge
Whether Bassanio had not once a love.[2]
Repent but you that you shall lose your friend,
And he repents not that he pays your debt;
For, if the Jew do cut but deep enough,
I'll pay it presently with all my heart.[3]

---

[1] on your charge: at your expense.
[2] love: friend.
[3] with all my heart: a jest that enhances the pathos of the scene.

BASSANIO.

Antonio, I am married to a wife
Which is as dear to me as life itself;
But life itself, my wife, and all the world,
Are not with me esteem'd above thy life:
I would lose all, ay, sacrifice them all
Here to this devil, to deliver you.

PORTIA.

Your wife would give you little thanks for that,
If she were by, to hear you make the offer.

GRATIANO.

I have a wife, whom, I protest, I love:
I would she were in heaven, so she could
Entreat some power to change this currish Jew.

NERISSA.

'Tis well you offer it behind her back;
The wish would make else an unquiet house.

SHYLOCK [aside].

These be the Christian husbands! I have a daughter;
Would any of the stock of Barabbas[1]
Had been her husband rather than a Christian!—
We trifle time:[2] I pray thee, pursue sentence.

PORTIA.

A pound of that same merchant's flesh is thine:
The court awards it, and the law doth give it.

SHYLOCK.

Most rightful judge!

PORTIA.

And you must cut this flesh from off his breast:
The law allows it, and the court awards it.

---

[1] Barabbas: a thief (Mark 15:6-11).
[2] We trifle time: we waste time with trivialities.

SHYLOCK.

Most learned judge!—A sentence! come, prepare!

PORTIA.

Tarry a little; there is something else.
This bond doth give thee here no jot[1] of blood,—
The words expressly are, 'a pound of flesh':
Take then thy bond, take thou thy pound of flesh;
But, in the cutting it, if thou dost shed
One drop of Christian blood, thy lands and goods
Are, by the laws of Venice, confiscate
Unto the state of Venice.

GRATIANO.

O upright judge!—Mark, Jew:—O learned judge!

SHYLOCK.

Is that the law?

PORTIA.

Thyself shalt see the act:
For, as thou urgest justice, be assured
Thou shalt have justice, more than thou desirest.

GRATIANO.

O learned judge!—Mark, Jew:—a learned judge!

SHYLOCK.

I take his offer, then;—pay the bond thrice,
And let the Christian go.

BASSANIO.

Here is the money.

PORTIA.

Soft!
The Jew shall have all justice;—soft! [2] no haste:—
He shall have nothing but the penalty.

GRATIANO.

O Jew! an upright judge, a learned judge!

---

[1] jot: iota; smallest particle.
[2] Soft: slowly.

PORTIA.

Therefore prepare thee to cut off the flesh.
Shed thou no blood; nor cut thou less nor more
But just a pound [1] of flesh: if thou cutt'st more
Or less than a just pound,—be it but so much
As makes it light or heavy in the substance,
Or the division of the twentieth part
Of one poor scruple, [2] nay, if the scale do turn
But in the estimation of a hair,—
Thou diest, and all thy goods are confiscate.

GRATIANO.

A second Daniel, a Daniel, Jew!
Now, infidel, I have you on the hip. [3]

PORTIA.

Why doth the Jew pause? take thy forfeiture.

SHYLOCK.

Give me my principal, and let me go.

BASSANIO.

I have it ready for thee; here it is.

PORTIA.

He hath refused it in the open court:
He shall have merely justice and his bond.

GRATIANO.

A Daniel, still say I, a second Daniel!—
I thank thee, Jew, for teaching me that word.

SHYLOCK.

Shall I not have barely my principal?

PORTIA.

Thou shalt have nothing but the forfeiture,
To be so taken at thy peril, Jew.

SHYLOCK.

Why, then the devil give him good of it!
I'll stay no longer question. [4]

---

[1] **just a pound**: an exact pound.
[2] **scruple**: a small unit of weight in ancient Rome.
[3] **I have you on the hip**: I have you at my mercy.
[4] **I'll stay no longer question**: I'll remain here no longer to be questioned.

PORTIA.

Tarry, Jew:

The law hath yet another hold on you.
It is enacted in the laws of Venice,—
If it be proved against an alien[1]
That by direct or indirect attempts
He seek the life of any citizen,
The party 'gainst the which he doth contrive
Shall seize one half his goods; the other half
Comes to the privy coffer of the state;
And the offender's life lies in the mercy
Of the duke only, 'gainst all other voice.[2]
In which predicament, I say, thou stand'st;
For it appears, by manifest[3] proceeding,
That indirectly, and directly too,
Thou hast contrived against the very life
Of the defendant; and thou hast incurr'd
The danger formerly by me rehearsed.[4]
Down, therefore, and beg mercy of the duke.

GRATIANO.

Beg that thou mayst have leave to hang thyself:
And yet, thy wealth being forfeit to the state,
Thou hast not left the value of a cord;[5]
Therefore thou must be hang'd at the state's charge.[6]

DUKE OF VENICE.

That thou shalt see the difference of our spirits,
I pardon thee thy life before thou ask it:
For half thy wealth, it is Antonio's;
The other half comes to the general state,
Which humbleness may drive unto a fine.[7]

PORTIA.

Ay, for the state,—not for Antonio.

---

[1] alien: non-Christian. [2] voice: jurisdiction. [3] manifest: evident. [4] rehearsed: enumerated. [5] cord: rope for hanging. [6] charge: expense.
[7] humbleness may drive unto a fine: if you repent and bear yourself humbly, this may be reduced to a mere fine.

SHYLOCK.

Nay, take my life and all; pardon not that:
You take my house, when you do take the prop[1]
That doth sustain my house; you take my life,
When you do take the means whereby I live.

PORTIA.

What mercy can you render him, Antonio?

GRATIANO.

A halter gratis;[2] nothing else, for God's sake.

ANTONIO.

So please my lord the duke and all the court
To quit[3] the fine for one half of his goods,
I am content; so he will let me have
The other half in use, to render it,
Upon his death, unto the gentleman
That lately stole his daughter:
Two things provided more,—that, for this favour,
He presently become a Christian;
The other, that he do record a gift,
Here in the court, of all he dies possest,
Unto his son Lorenzo and his daughter.

DUKE OF VENICE.

He shall do this; or else I do recant
The pardon that I late pronounced here.

PORTIA.

Art thou contented, Jew? what dost thou say?

SHYLOCK.

I am content.

PORTIA.

                Clerk, draw a deed of gift.

---

[1] prop: wealth.
[2] halter gratis: a free rope.
[3] quit: satisfy.

SHYLOCK.

I pray you, give me leave to go from hence;
I am not well: send the deed after me,
And I will sign it.

DUKE OF VENICE.

               Get thee gone, but do it.

GRATIANO.

In christening shalt thou have two godfathers:
Had I been judge, thou shouldst have had ten more,[1]
To bring thee to the gallows, not the font.   [*Exit* SHYLOCK.

DUKE OF VENICE.

Sir, I entreat you home with me to dinner.

PORTIA.

I humbly do desire your Grace of pardon:
I must away this night toward Padua,
And it is meet I presently set forth.

DUKE OF VENICE.

I am sorry that your leisure serves you not.[2]—
Antonio, gratify[3] this gentleman;
For, in my mind, you are much bound to him.

                [*Exeunt* DUKE *and his* TRAIN.

BASSANIO.

Most worthy gentleman, I and my friend
Have by your wisdom been this day acquitted
Of grievous penalties; in lieu whereof
Three thousand ducats, due unto the Jew,
We freely cope your courteous pains[4] withal.

ANTONIO.

And stand indebted, over and above,
In love and service to you evermore.

---

[1] **thou shouldst have had ten more:** you would have had ten more men; that is, a jury of twelve men. [2] **your leisure serves you not:** you do not have the time at your disposal. [3] **gratify:** reward. [4] **We freely cope your courteous pains:** we freely offer repayment for your courteous services.

PORTIA.

He is well paid that is well satisfied;
And I, delivering[1] you, am satisfied,
And therein do account myself well paid:
My mind was never yet more mercenary.
I pray you, know me when we meet again:
I wish you well, and so I take my leave.

BASSANIO.

Dear sir, of force I must attempt you further:[2]
Take some remembrance of us, as a tribute,
Not as a fee: grant me two things, I pray you,—
Not to deny me, and to pardon me.

PORTIA.

You press me far, and therefore I will yield.
[to ANTONIO] Give me your gloves, I'll wear them for your
    sake;
[to BASSANIO] And, for your love, I'll take this ring from
    you;—
Do not draw back your hand; I'll take no more;
And you in love shall not deny me this.

BASSANIO.

This ring, good sir,—alas, it is a trifle!
I will not shame myself to give[3] you this.

PORTIA.

I will have nothing else but only this;
And now methinks I have a mind to it.

BASSANIO.

There's more depends on this than on the value,
The dearest ring in Venice will I give you,
And find it out by proclamation:
Only for this, I pray you, pardon me.

---

[1] delivering: saving.
[2] of force I must attempt you further: I am forced to try to pre-
vail on you again.
[3] to give: by giving.

PORTIA.

I see, sir, you are liberal in offers:
You taught me first to beg; and now methinks
You teach me how a beggar should be answer'd.

BASSANIO.

Good sir, this ring was given me by my wife;
And, when she put it on, she made me vow
That I should neither sell nor give nor lose it.

PORTIA.

That 'scuse[1] serves many men to save their gifts.
An if your wife be not a mad-woman,
And know how well I have deserved this ring,
She would not hold out enemy for ever
For giving it to me. Well, peace be with you!

[*Exeunt* PORTIA *and* NERISSA.

ANTONIO.

My Lord Bassanio, let him have the ring:
Let his deservings, and my love withal,[2]
Be valued 'gainst your wife's commandment.

BASSANIO.

Go, Gratiano, run and overtake him;
Give him this ring; and bring him, if thou canst,
Unto Antonio's house:—away! make haste.   [*Exit* GRATIANO.
Come, you and I will thither presently;[3]
And in the morning early will we both
Fly toward Belmont: come, Antonio.   [*Exeunt.*

---

[1] 'scuse: excuse.
[2] withal: at the same time.
[3] presently: at once.

Scene II.

The same. A street.

Enter PORTIA *and* NERISSA.

PORTIA.

Inquire the Jew's house out, give him this deed,
And let him sign it: we'll away to-night,
And be a day before our husbands home:
This deed will be well welcome to Lorenzo.

Enter GRATIANO.

GRATIANO.

Fair sir, you are well o'erta'en:[1]
My Lord Bassanio, upon more advice,[2]
Hath sent you here this ring; and doth entreat
Your company at dinner.

PORTIA.

That cannot be:
His ring I do accept most thankfully;
And so, I pray you, tell him: furthermore,
I pray you, show my youth old Shylock's house.

GRATIANO.

That will I do.

NERISSA.

Sir, I would speak with you.—
to PORTIA] I'll see if I can get my husband's ring,
Which I did make him swear to keep for ever.

PORTIA [*to* NERISSA].

Thou mayst, I warrant. We shall have old swearing[3]
That they did give the rings away to men;
But we'll outface them, and outswear them too.—
Away! make haste: thou know'st where I will tarry.

NERISSA.

Come, good sir, will you show me to this house?   [*Exeunt.*

---

[1] **you are well o'erta'en:** I am lucky to have overtaken you.
[2] **upon more advice:** on further reflection, or consideration.
[3] **old swearing:** abundant or great swearing.

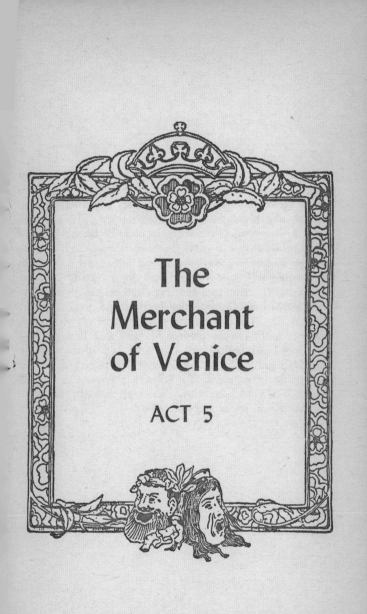

The Merchant of Venice

ACT 5

ACT V

In Belmont, Lorenzo and Jessica talk together in a moonlit night. They are interrupted by a messenger who tells them that Portia is returning. Launcelot enter⸱ ᵃ informs them that his master will be back before morning. To welcome Portia, Lorenzo orders musicians to play. Portia and Nerissa arrive; before they can enter the house they hear Bassanio's trumpet. Bassanio greets his wife and introduces Antonio to her; Portia's welcome is interrupted by a quarrel between Nerissa and Gratiano over the ring Gratiano has given away. Portia learns from Gratiano that her husband, too, has given away his ring. The mock quarrel, with its bawdy overtones, continues until Antonio pledges his soul that Bassanio will nevermore break faith. Portia then tells them of the disguise and adds more joy by telling Antonio that three of his ships have suddenly returned. To Lorenzo she gives the deed signed by Shylock, and then invites all into the house to continue the questions and storytelling.

ACT V. SCENE I.

Belmont. Avenue to PORTIA's *house.*

Enter LORENZO *and* JESSICA.

LORENZO.

The moon shines bright:—in such a night as this,
When the sweet wind did gently kiss the trees,
And they did make no noise,—in such a night
Troilus[1] methinks mounted the Troyan[2] walls,
And sigh'd his soul toward the Grecian tents,
Where Cressid [3] lay that night.

JESSICA.

      In such a night
Did Thisbe[4] fearfully o'ertrip the dew,
And saw the lion's shadow ere himself,
And ran dismay'd away.

LORENZO.

    In such a night
Stood Dido[5] with a willow[6] in her hand
Upon the wild sea-banks, and waft her love
To come again to Carthage.

JESSICA.

     In such a night
Medea[7] gather'd the enchanted herbs
That did renew old Aeson.[8]

LORENZO.

     In such a night
Did Jessica steal from the wealthy Jew,
And with an unthrift[9] love did run from Venice
As far as Belmont.

JESSICA.

    In such a night

---

[1] **Troilus:** son of Priam, King of Troy. [2] **Troyan:** Trojan. [3] **Cressid:** Cressida; the faithless love of Troilus. [4] **Thisbe:** the fairest maiden of Babylonia whose sweetheart, Pyramus, thought she had been devoured by a lion and killed himself. [5] **Dido:** Queen of Carthage, in love with Aeneas. [6] **willow:** symbol of sadness or misery. [7] **Medea:** daughter of the King of Colchis, in love with Jason. [8] **Aeson:** father of Jason. [9] **unthrift:** regardless of worldly possessions.

Did young Lorenzo swear he loved her well,
Stealing her soul with many vows of faith,
And ne'er a true one.

LORENZO.

In such a night
Did pretty Jessica, like a little shrew,
Slander her love, and he forgave it her.

JESSICA.

I would out-night you,[1] did no body come:
But, hark, I hear the footing[2] of a man.

Enter STEPHANO.

LORENZO.

Who comes so fast in silence of the night?

STEPHANO.

A friend.

LORENZO.

A friend! what friend? your name, I pray you, friend?

STEPHANO.

Stephano is my name; and I bring word
My mistress will before the break of day
Be here at Belmont: she doth stray about
By holy crosses,[3] where she kneels and prays
For happy wedlock hours.

LORENZO.

Who comes with her?

STEPHANO.

None but a holy hermit and her maid.
I pray you, is my master yet return'd?

LORENZO.

He is not, nor we have not heard from him.—
But go we in, I pray thee, Jessica,

---

[1] **I would out-night you:** I would win over you in such a contest;
that is, phrases beginning "in such a night." [2] **footing:** footsteps.
[3] **doth stray about/By Holy crosses:** makes pilgrimages from one
sacred shrine to another: these shrines, which marked the place
where heroes or saints were born, or travelers died, were usually
on tops of hills or at the intersections of roads.

And ceremoniously let us prepare[1]
Some welcome for the mistress of the house.

Enter LAUNCELOT.

    LAUNCELOT GOBBO.
Sola, sola! wo ha, ho! sola, sola!
    LORENZO.
Who calls?
    LAUNCELOT GOBBO.
Sola!—did you see Master Lorenzo? Master
Lorenzo!—sola, sola!
    LORENZO.
Leave hollaing, man:—here.
    LAUNCELOT GOBBO.
Sola!—where? where?
    LORENZO.
Here.
    LAUNCELOT GOBBO.
Tell him there's a post[2] come from my master, with his horn
full of good news: my master will be here ere morning. [*Exit*.
    LORENZO.
Sweet soul, let's in, and there expect their coming.
And yet no matter:—why should we go in?—
My friend Stephano, signify, I pray you,
Within the house, your mistress is at hand;
And bring your music forth into the air.   [*Exit* STEPHANO.
How sweet the moonlight sleeps upon this bank!
Here will we sit, and let the sounds of music
Creep in our ears: soft stillness and the night
Become the touches of sweet harmony.[3]

---

[1] **ceremoniously let us prepare:** let us prepare some ceremonious welcome.
[2] **post:** messenger.
[3] **touches of sweet harmony:** the hand on a musical instrument.

Sit, Jessica. Look; how the floor of heaven
Is thick inlaid with patines[1] of bright gold:
There's not the smallest orb which thou behold'st
But in his motion like an angel sings,
Still quiring[2] to the young-eyed cherubins,—
Such harmony is in immortal souls;
But whilst this muddy vesture of decay[3]
Doth grossly close it in, we cannot hear it.

Enter MUSICIANS.

Come, ho, and wake Diana with a hymn!
With sweetest touches pierce your mistress' ear,
And draw her home with music.   [*Music plays.*
     JESSICA.
I am never merry when I hear sweet music.
     LORENZO.
The reason is, your spirits are attentive:
For do but note a wild and wanton[4] herd,
Or race of youthful and unhandled [5] colts,
Fetching mad bounds, bellowing, and neighing loud,
Which is the hot condition of their blood;
If they but hear perchance a trumpet sound,
Or any air of music touch their ears,
You shall perceive them make a mutual stand,[6]
Their savage eyes turn'd to a modest[7] gaze,
By the sweet power of music: therefore the poet
Did feign that Orpheus[8] drew trees, stones, and floods;
Since naught so stockish,[9] hard, and full of rage,
But music for the time doth change his nature.
The man that hath no music in himself,

---

[1] patines: patterns. [2] quiring: choiring. [3] muddy vesture of decay:
this clothing of mortal flesh. [4] wanton: untrained. [5] unhandled:
unbroken. [6] mutual stand: all stand still. [7] modest: restrained;
tamed. [8] Orpheus: the son of Apollo and the Muse Calliope; when
he played on his lyre, he charmed wild beasts and even the trees
and stones were softened. [9] stockish: like a block of wood; stolid.

Nor is not moved with concord of sweet sounds,
Is fit for treasons, stratagems,[1] and spoils;
The motions of his spirit are dull as night,
And his affections dark as Erebus:[2]
Let no such man be trusted.—Mark the music.

Enter PORTIA *and* NERISSA.

PORTIA.

That light we see is burning in my hall.
How far that little candle throws his beams!
So shines a good deed in a naughty[3] world.

NERISSA.

When the moon shone, we did not see the candle.

PORTIA.

So doth the greater glory dim the less:
A substitute shines brightly as a king,
Until a king be by; and then his state
Empties itself, as doth an inland brook
Into the main of waters.[4]—Music! hark!

NERISSA.

It is your music, madam, of the house.

PORTIA.

Nothing is good, I see, without respect:
Methinks it sounds much sweeter than by day.

NERISSA.

Silence bestows that virtue on it, madam.

PORTIA.

The crow doth sing as sweetly as the lark,
When neither is attended;[5] and I think
The nightingale, if she should sing by day,
When every goose is cackling, would be thought
No better a musician than the wren.
How many things by season season'd are[6]

---

[1] stratagems: dark and evil deeds. [2] Erebus: in Greek mythology, the gloomy underground region through which souls passed on their way to Hades. [3] naughty: wicked; evil. [4] main of waters: ocean; sea. [5] attended: accompanied (competed with). [6] by season season'd are: timeliness gives an advantage to any action.

To their right praise and true perfection!—
Peace, ho! the moon sleeps with Endymion,[1]
And would not be awaked.   [*Music ceases.*

LORENZO.

                    That is the voice,
Or I am much deceived, of Portia.

PORTIA.

He knows me, as the blind man knows the cuckoo,
By the bad voice.

LORENZO.

                    Dear lady, welcome home.

PORTIA.

We have been praying for our husbands' health,
Which speed,[2] we hope, the better for our words.
Are they return'd?

LORENZO.

                    Madam, they are not yet;
But there is come a messenger before,
To signify their coming.

PORTIA.

                    Go in, Nerissa;
Give orders to my servants that they take
No note at all of our being absent hence;—
Nor you, Lorenzo;—Jessica, nor you   [*A tucket sounds.*

LORENZO.

Your husband is at hand; I hear his trumpet:
We are no tell-tales, madam; fear you not.

PORTIA.

This night methinks is but the daylight sick;
It looks a little paler: 'tis a day,
Such as the day is when the sun is hid.

---

[1] **Endymion:** a beautiful young shepherd whom Diana (or Selene),
the moon goddess, fell in love with and watched over while he
slept with his flock on Mount Latmos.
[2] **speed:** prosper.

Enter BASSANIO, ANTONIO, GRATIANO, *and their* FOLLOWERS.

BASSANIO.

We should hold day with the Antipodes,

If you would walk in absence of the sun.[1]

PORTIA.

Let me give light, but let me not be light;[2]

For a light wife doth make a heavy[3] husband,

And never be Bassanio so for me:

But God sort all!—You're welcome home, my lord.

BASSANIO.

I thank you, madam. Give welcome to my friend.

This is the man, this is Antonio,

To whom I am so infinitely bound.

PORTIA.

You should in all sense[4] be much bound to him,

For, as I hear, he was much bound for you.

ANTONIO.

No more than I am well acquitted of.

PORTIA.

Sir, you are very welcome to our house:

It must appear in other ways than words,

Therefore I scant this breathing courtesy.[5]

GRATIANO [*to* NERISSA].

By yonder moon I swear you do me wrong;

In faith, I gave it to the judge's clerk:

Would he were gelt[6] that had it, for my part,

Since you do take it, love, so much at heart.

PORTIA.

A quarrel, ho, already! what's the matter?

GRATIANO.

About a hoop of gold, a paltry ring

---

[1] **We should hold day with the Antipodes/ If you would walk in absence of the sun**: it would be day here when the sun is shining on the other side of the world (Antipodes) because your beauty shines like the sun. [2] **light**: flighty; unfaithful. [3] **heavy**: sad. [4] **You should in all sense**: there is every reason why you should. [5] **scant this breathing courtesy**: cut short this wordy politeness. [6] **gelt**: gelded.

That she did give to me; whose posy[1] was
For all the world like cutler's poetry
Upon a knife, 'Love me, and leave me not.'

NERISSA.

What talk you of the posy or the value?
You swore to me, when I did give it you,
That you would wear it till your hour of death;
And that it should lie with you in your grave:
Though not for me, yet for your vehement oaths,
You should have been respective,[2] and have kept it.
Gave it a judge's clerk! no, God's my judge,
The clerk will ne'er wear hair on's face that had it.

GRATIANO.

He will, an if he live to be a man.

NERISSA.

Ay, if a woman live to be a man.

GRATIANO.

Now, by this hand, I gave it to a youth,—
A kind of boy; a little scrubbed[3] boy,
No higher than thyself, the judge's clerk;
A prating[4] boy, that begg'd it as a fee:
I could not for my heart deny it him.

PORTIA.

You were to blame,—I must be plain with you,—
To part so slightly with your wife's first gift;
A thing stuck on with oaths upon your finger,
And so riveted with faith unto your flesh.
I gave my love a ring, and made him swear
Never to part with it; and here he stands,—
I dare be sworn for him, he would not leave it,
Nor pluck it from his finger, for the wealth
That the world masters. Now, in faith, Gratiano,

---

[1] posy: poetic inscription on the inside of the ring.
[2] respective: mindful.
[3] scrubbed: stunted, like a scrub oak; young stripling.
[4] prating: babbling; boastful.

You give your wife too unkind a cause of grief:
An 'twere to me,[1] I should be mad [2] at it.

  BASSANIO [*aside*].

Why, I were best[3] to cut my left hand off,
And swear I lost the ring defending it.

  GRATIANO.

My Lord Bassanio gave his ring away
Unto the judge that begg'd it, and indeed
Deserved it too; and then the boy, his clerk,
That took some pains in writing,[4] he begg'd mine:
And neither man nor master would take aught
But the two rings.

  PORTIA.

     What ring gave you, my lord?
Not that, I hope, which you received of me.

  BASSANIO.

If I could add a lie unto a fault,
I would deny it; but you see my finger
Hath not the ring upon it,—it is gone.

  PORTIA.

Even so void is your false heart of truth.
By heaven, I will ne'er come in your bed
Until I see the ring.

  NERISSA.

     Nor I in yours
Till I again see mine.

  BASSANIO.

     Sweet Portia,
If you did know to whom I gave the ring,
If you did know for whom I gave the ring,
And would conceive[5] for what I gave the ring,
And how unwillingly I left the ring,

---

[1] An 'twere to me: and if it were I.
[2] mad: furious.
[3] I were best: it would have been better for me.
[4] took some pains in writing: performed some service as a scribe and deserved pay for it.
[5] conceive: understand perfectly.

When naught would be accepted but the ring,
You would abate[1] the strength of your displeasure.

PORTIA.

If you had known the virtue of the ring,
Or half her worthiness that gave the ring,
Or your own honour to contain[2] the ring,
You would not then have parted with the ring.
What man is there so much unreasonable,
If you had pleased to have defended it
With any terms of zeal, wanted the modesty[3]
To urge the thing held as a ceremony? [4]
Nerissa teaches me what to believe:
I'll die for't[5] but some woman had the ring.

BASSANIO.

No, by my honour, madam, by my soul,
No woman had it, but a civil doctor,[6]
Which did refuse three thousand ducats of me,
And begg'd the ring; the which I did deny him,
And suffer'd him to go displeased away;
Even he that did uphold the very life
Of my dear friend. What should I say, sweet lady?
I was enforced to send it after him:
I was beset with shame and courtesy;
My honour would not let ingratitude
So much besmear it. Pardon me, good lady;
For, by these blessed candles of the night,
Had you been there, I think, you would have begg'd
The ring of me to give the worthy doctor.

PORTIA.

Let not that doctor e'er come near my house:
Since he hath got the jewel that I loved,

---

[1] abate: lessen; temper. [2] contain: keep; retain. [3] wanted the modesty: lacked the prudence. [4] To urge the thing held as a ceremony: to insist upon the ring being considered as a sacred pledge. [5] I'll die for't: I'll wager my life on it. [6] civil doctor: doctor of civil law (lawyer).

And that which you did swear to keep for me,
I will become as liberal as you;
I'll not deny him any thing I have,
No, not my body nor my husband's bed:
Know him I shall, I am well sure of it:
Lie not a night from home; watch me like Argus:[1]
If you do not, if I be left alone,
Now, by mine honour, which is yet mine own,
I'll have that doctor for my bedfellow.

NERISSA.

And I his clerk; therefore be well advised [2]
How you do leave me to mine own protection.

GRATIANO.

Well, do you so: let not me take him, then;
For if I do, I'll mar the young clerk's pen.

ANTONIO.

I am the unhappy subject of these quarrels.

PORTIA.

Sir, grieve not you; you are welcome notwithstanding.

BASSANIO.

Portia, forgive me this enforced wrong;[3]
And, in the hearing of these many friends,
I swear to thee, even by thine own fair eyes,
Wherein I see myself.—

PORTIA.

Mark you but that!
In both my eyes he doubly[4] sees himself;
In each eye, one:—swear by your double self,
And there's an oath of credit.[5]

BASSANIO.

Nay, but hear me:

---

[1] Argus: in Greek mythology, a monster in human shape with a hundred eyes, some of which were always awake.
[2] be well advised: be warned.
[3] enforced wrong: this wrongful thing that I was forced to do.
[4] doubly: used in a bad sense; full of duplicity.
[5] an oath of credit: an oath that may be believed.

Pardon this fault, and by my soul I swear
I never more will break an oath with thee.

ANTONIO.

I once did lend my body for his wealth;[1]
Which, but for him that had your husband's ring,
Had quite miscarried: I dare be bound again,
My soul upon the forfeit, that your lord
Will never more break faith advisedly.[2]

PORTIA.

Then you shall be his surety. Give him this;
And bid him keep it better than the other.

ANTONIO.

Here, Lord Bassanio; swear to keep this ring.

BASSANIO.

By heaven, it is the same I gave the doctor!

PORTIA.

I had it of him; pardon me, Bassanio;
For, by this ring, the doctor lay with me.

NERISSA.

And pardon me, my gentle Gratiano;
For that same scrubbed boy, the doctor's clerk,
In lieu of this, last night did lie with me.

GRATIANO.

Why, this is like the mending of highways
In summer, where the ways are fair enough:
What, are we cuckolds ere we have deserved it?

PORTIA.

Speak not so grossly.—You are all amazed:
Here is a letter, read it at your leisure;
It comes from Padua, from Bellario:
There you shall find that Portia was the doctor;

---

[1] **for his wealth:** to make him rich.
[2] **advisedly:** deliberately.

Nerissa there her clerk: Lorenzo here
Shall witness I set forth as soon as you,
And even but now return'd; I have not yet
Enter'd my house.—Antonio, you are welcome;
And I have better news in store for you
Than you expect: unseal this letter soon;
There you shall find three of your argosies
Are richly come to harbour suddenly:
You shall not know by what strange accident
I chanced on this letter.

ANTONIO.

I am dumb.

BASSANIO.

Were you the doctor, and I knew you not?

GRATIANO.

Were you the clerk that is to make me cuckold?

NERISSA.

Ay, but the clerk that never means to do it,
Unless he live until he be a man.

BASSANIO.

Sweet doctor, you shall be my bedfellow:
When I am absent, then lie with my wife.

ANTONIO.

Sweet lady, you have given me life and living;
For here I read for certain that my ships
Are safely come to road.[1]

PORTIA.

How now, Lorenzo!
My clerk hath some good comforts too for you.

NERISSA.

Ay, and I'll give them him without a fee.—
There do I give to you and Jessica,

---

[1] safely come to road: are safely anchored (road means "anchor-age").

From the rich Jew, a special deed of gift,
After his death, of all he dies possest of.

   LORENZO.

Fair ladies, you drop manna in the way
of starved people.

   PORTIA.

      It is almost morning,
And yet I am sure you are not satisfied
Of these events at full. Let us go in;
And charge us there upon inter'gatories,[1]
And we will answer all things faithfully.

   GRATIANO.

Let it be so: the first inter'gatory
That my Nerissa shall be sworn on is,
Whether till the next night she had rather stay,
Or go to bed now, being two hours to day:
But were the day come, I should wish it dark,
That I were couching with the doctor's clerk.
Well, while I live I'll fear no other thing
So sore[2] as keeping safe Nerissa's ring.   [*Exeunt.*

---

[1] **charge us there upon inter'gatories:** in certain courts, when a
complaint was made against a person for "contempt," before sen-
tencing, the defendant was sent into the Crown's office and,
"charged upon interrogatories," swore that he would "answer all
things faithfully."

[2] **so sore:** so intensely.